Graphic Design Process
From Problem to Solution
20 Case Studies

LAURENCE KING

Published in 2012 by
Laurence King Publishing Ltd
361–363 City Road
London EC1V 1LR
United Kingdom

Tel. +44 (0)20 7841 6900
Fax + 44 (0)20 7841 6910
enquiries@laurenceking.com
www.laurenceking.com

Text and design © 2011
Nancy Skolos and Thomas Wedell

This book was produced by Laurence
King Publishing Ltd, London

A catalogue record for this book is
available from the British Library

ISBN: 978-1-85669-826-9

Design by Skolos Wedell

Typeset in Akzidenz-Grotesk, designed
by Hermann Berthold, Berthold LLC, and
Dispatch, designed by Cyrus Highsmith,
The Font Bureau, Inc.

Printed in China

Nancy Skolos and Thomas Wedell

Graphic Design Process
From Problem to Solution
20 Case Studies

Laurence King Publishing

contents

introduction

Graphic Design Process offers a detailed investigation into the activity of graphic design—a field that spans many media, offers exposure to endless subject material, and reaches into countless other disciplines for inspiration. This book is a reflection of the joy we get from doing our own graphic design work: watching an idea gradually take shape, engaging in a back-and-forth with it, and reaching a resolution.

Insights into process amplify the meaning of creative work. The musings of those practitioners willing to share their thoughts and experiences enlighten and inspire us, often providing a sense of deep affinity, validation, and motivation. Our goal in putting this book together was to curate a discussion about the creative process in contemporary graphic design that would invigorate students and professional designers in the same way.

This collection of twenty case studies features a selection of designers who have visible, carefully developed methodologies. Drawing on a range of approaches, each designer affirms that there is no single way to conduct a design practice, and that every project demands its own way of working.

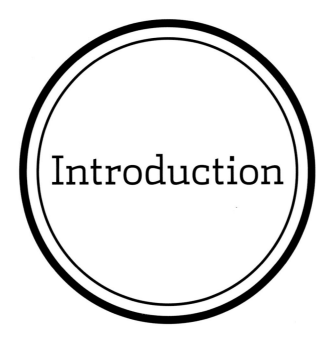

Introduction

While the design process is seldom linear, for the purposes of examining the topic, we have constructed a chronological model: beginning with preliminary steps in the chapters 'Research' and 'Inspiration' and progressing to strategies and techniques for actualizing ideas in 'Drawing,' 'Narrative,' 'Abstraction,' and 'Development.' The book's concluding chapter, 'Collaboration,' looks at the valuable ways in which design practice is enhanced through partnerships both within and outside the field. Our aim isn't to prescribe a definitive methodology, but to research the highest level of thinking at every stage of the process.

Each case study concentrates on either a single design or a thematically based selection of projects. Some issues were better served by an in-depth analysis of one problem, while other topics required a broader sampling. Visual form varies greatly among the designers, but a common denominator in all projects is an open-endedness in the visual language that extends the design process by engaging the audience.

It may be assumed that there are some innate talents or behaviors, or characteristic work styles, that all gifted designers share that enable them to solve complex problems. However, in interviewing the designers featured here, we could identify only a few predictable common threads in their experiences: the busier a designer is, the more ideas mix in the mind for inventive solutions; ideas usually come when a designer least expects them; and exposure to visual art at a young age, through a relative, teacher, or friend, opened a path to design.

If there is any pattern to design processes, it is the result of inherent constraints on design projects. Even though, on the surface, mundane limitations such as time and budget would appear to run counter to the act of creativity, it is these very restraints that stimulate inventive solutions. Engaging with a problem through extended research and analysis, in combination with a personal perspective and a tendency toward risk taking, informs a unique process that not only results in a solution to the problem at hand but also builds new insights that can advance future projects.

Over the years, graphic design has moved through many visual and technical trends. Some tendencies remain part of the design landscape, but many fade away. This book celebrates the experience of making the work, which, at the end of the day, is the biggest reward.

research

1.1 The Design Brief
A2/SW/HK, London

1.2 Mapping/Modeling
Dubberly Design Office, San Francisco

1.3 The Client
Johnson Banks, London

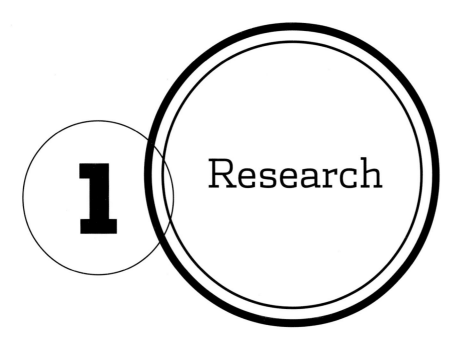

1 Research

Understanding a project's context through research is of foremost importance in the design process. Although it is often tempting for the designer to focus on the formal aspects of an assignment, it is equally important to identify the systems within which the project will operate as well as the outside forces that might impact the project's ultimate effectiveness.

The following case studies, 'The Design Brief,' 'Mapping/ Modeling,' and 'The Client,' look at important strategies that lay the groundwork for meaningful engagement with complex design problems.

A design brief is a detailed description of an assignment generated by the client and/or the designer, or worked on in collaboration by both parties. It spells out the aims of the project, including its targeted audience, possible lifespan, and overall objectives; it also details constraints, such as budget and deadlines, and often anticipates future considerations.

A concept map is a model generated to gain in-depth insight into the problem at hand. The designer/design team examines the project both objectively and sub-jectively in order to tease out connections between the project and its related systems—exhausting all possible associations. These models not only foster a comprehen-sive understanding of the assignment, but also generate visual artifacts that facilitate the sharing of ideas among the collaborators.[1]

While research is a logical place to begin our sequence of case studies, it is important to keep in mind that the design process is iterative. Analysis works hand in hand with sketching and rapid prototyping to facilitate a pro-ductive feedback loop between designer and client/user.[2] Maintaining an informed dialogue with the client com-missioning the work forges a strong partnership that is fundamental to the success of the entire project.

1. Interview with Hugh Dubberly, November 2010.
2. Ibid.

A2/SW/HK

The Design Brief

For Scott Williams and Henrik Kubel of A2/SW/HK, creativity is a clear process that originates from the client's brief and evolves skillfully through a sequence of logical decisions. Says Kubel, 'Most of our work has an idea behind it that makes sense…there's the starting point and there needs to be a direction, a concept; not a pun or a cliché but something that's useful, practical, and appropriate. Each project has a purpose, a mission, and every part is critical.…The design brief is key to defining the opportunities and limitations of a project, both of which are equally important in discovering the best solution. The process begins with the initial conversation with the client and then becomes an obsession.'

One excellent example is the 'reading room' A2 designed for the Turner Prize exhibition at Tate Britain in 2002—the exit point of the show, where the audience could leave comments, read the artist books, and watch artist interviews. The Turner Prize is awarded annually to a British contemporary artist. The four artists shortlisted for the prize are featured in the exhibition, which always generates public debate. Because of this, the Tate asked A2 to design an additional gallery as the final space in the exhibition to provide a place that would open a dialogue with the public audience and seek their opinions. Key elements of the brief were that the gallery had to be: an interpretive, contextual space; a fifth room that flowed seamlessly out of the other four; an open gallery of 9 x 9 meters (29.5 x 29.5 feet); built from transportable components that could be reused for up to five years. The museum gave A2 an exact production budget and six to eight weeks to come back with a solution.

'The design brief is key to defining the opportunities and limitations of a project, both of which are equally important in discovering the best solution.'

A2/SW/HK's design for a
final gallery in the Turner Prize
exhibition at Tate Britain invites
public participation.

'Once you have the conversation
and the brief, there is no particular
method but one based on life and
on knowledge.'

The brief's requirement for a transportable, reusable gallery led A2 in the direction of a modular design, beginning with a system of wall panels carefully designed to fit the space as well as work within the available sheet sizes of materials. Foam-board prototypes were built to test the size of the components and determine the most unified and economical way to combine them.

Ergonomics and the limits of the human reach naturally dictated the positioning of the comment area, which found its place around the perimeter of the room, with comment cards also becoming a modular design element. The design logic behind the cards is a compact example of A2's incisive distillation process.

Beginning with postal regulations, A2 decided that the comment cards should be the size of a regular postcard. As if to underscore the act of public participation, the pencils did double duty as pegs that fastened the cards to the walls, piercing the cards through the o in 'comment'; the word was sized and placed so that the o was in the center and the card balanced squarely on the pencil. The text was set in the museum's Tate typeface; the color of the text matched the wall color, which would be changed each year.

Contemporary art, especially conceptual art, is a critical influence on the way A2 approaches their design work. Its presence is evident in this exhibit design, which is itself like a piece of conceptual art— with the design brief as its concept and its physical manifestation completely supporting the hypothesis. Ironically, they do not want to be considered artists. Williams asserts, 'We're not artists and we have no aspirations to be.'

'If we didn't have six weeks on this, we'd probably still be working on it now...the deadline is something to work against—part of that crazy process; it forces you to stop working.'

The comment postcards were an integral part of the modular system that spanned the perimeter of the audience-participation space.

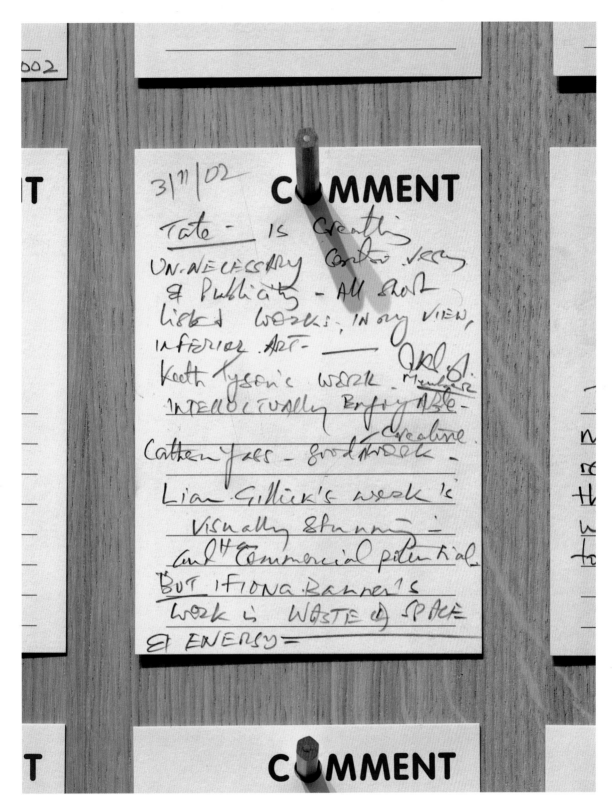

The mailing size of the comment cards, the use of the pencil as a fastener, and the position of the word 'comment' were all interdependent design decisions that supported the brief's goal of audience participation.

For the exhibition *Ergonomics—Real Design* at the Design Museum in London, A2 worked in collaboration with exhibition architect Michael Marriot to develop the identity, applied graphics, online graphics, and printed material. The primary directive of the brief was 'To create a strong exhibition identity that communicated and translated the theme of ergonomics in design, in a clear and concise way, to a large audience.'

To convey the subject of ergonomics clearly, all the design considerations, such as scale and visibility, were based on human factors. For example, the yellow and black color palette, which was homogeneously applied to all walls, exhibition stands, and graphics, was informed by the highly legible color combinations often used for public signage systems in airports or on roads.

Both of the typefaces used in the exhibition—Ergonomics and New Rail Alphabet—were designed by the studio. Ergonomics was designed specifically for the exhibition, and New Rail Alphabet was designed in collaboration with Margaret Calvert and is an adaptation of the typeface Calvert designed in 1965 for British Railways.

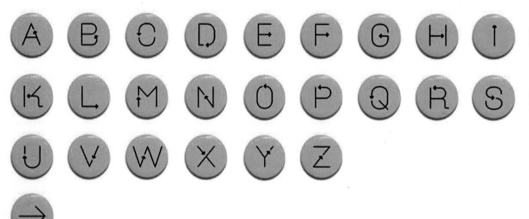

The bespoke typeface Ergonomics activated the theme of the exhibition by using arrows to direct the viewer's eye through the anatomy of each letter.

Exhibition identity, applied graphics, and brochure, including original display typeface, for *Ergonomics—Real Design*, Design Museum, London.

Exhibition design by Michael Marriot.

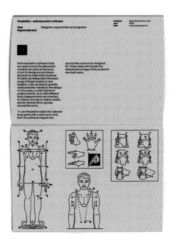

Creative DNA
A2/SW/HK

A2/SW/HK is an independent design studio based in London. Formed by Royal College of Art graduates Scott Williams and Henrik Kubel in 2000, A2/SW/HK work with national and international clients on design consultancy, art direction, identity, publishing, exhibitions, website design, and the creation of unique typefaces for all media. Williams and Kubel are members of the Alliance Graphique Internationale.

In 2009, Williams and Kubel established A2-Type to release and distribute over a decade's worth of their specially crafted typefaces. A2-Type create and release retail typefaces at regular intervals, as well as developing bespoke fonts for magazines, newspapers, brands, etc. Clients include the Museum of Modern Art, New York; Tate Modern, Tate Britain, the V&A Museum, and the Design Museum, London; Royal College of Art, London; Penguin Books; Phaidon Press; Faber & Faber; *Wallpaper** magazine; and Royal Mail.

Dubberly Design Office

Mapping/Modeling

Hugh Dubberly and his firm, Dubberly Design Office (DDO), known for their critical thinking in the world of contemporary design practice, are strong advocates for strategic planning. Dubberly outlines a range of mapping systems that his team works with: 'concept maps, which explore big ideas, present research, and stand alone, often as posters; working models, which show user goals and tasks, technology systems, and business processes, and reflect what we learn about a project's context; and task-flow maps, which document existing software, processes, and services, or illustrate proposals for new ones.' Some maps are part of a larger design while others are visualizations of processes that are used as teaching tools.

'If we wish to improve our products, we must improve our processes; we must continually redesign not just our products but also the way we design.'

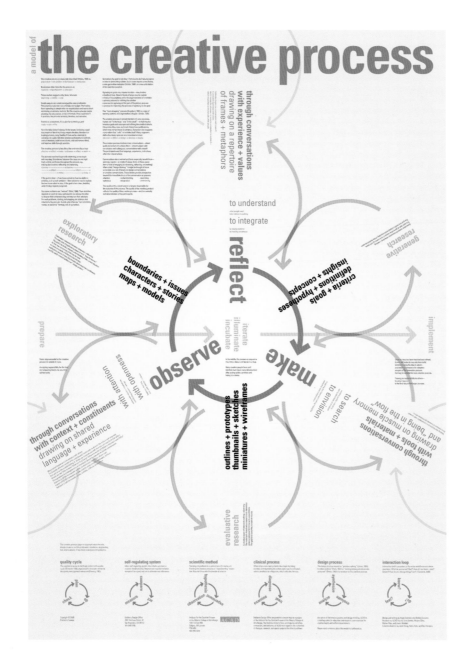

Above: Modular white boards in the DDO office are in a continuous state of flux.

An extensive and well-organized library supports DDO's passion for research.

Left: *A Model of the Creative Process*, part of a series of concept maps designed for the Alberta College of Art and Design.

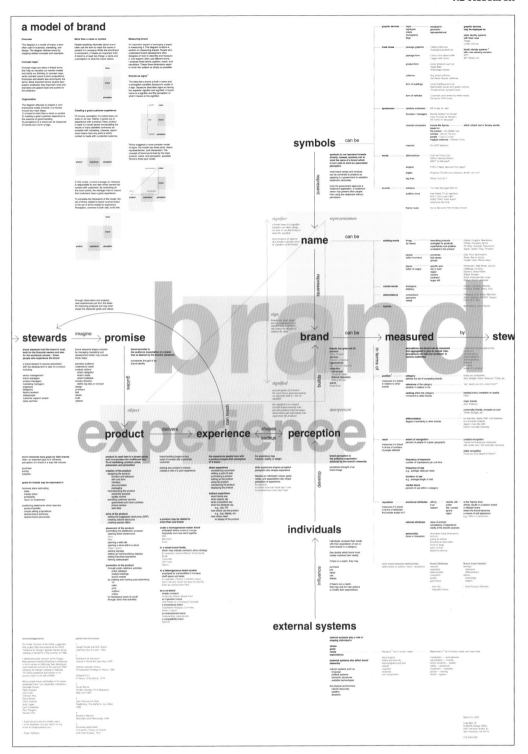

A Model of Brand, a concept map designed for the American Institute of Graphic Arts.

In 2006, the Alberta College of Art and Design commissioned DDO to develop a series of concept maps on the theme of 'Innovation, Play, and the Creative Process' to mark the opening of their new Center for the Creative Process. DDO collaborated with faculty to diagram 'very big and abstract design ideas,' Dubberly explains. The resulting posters, such as A Model of the Creative Process, are both visually striking and cerebral.

Another concept map, A Model of Brand, designed for the American Institute of Graphic Arts, shows how mapping can expand awareness of seemingly familiar concepts. The term 'brand' has been invoked since the mid-1990s to describe an upgraded version of corporate identity—one that can support a distinctive character for a particular company or organization and also span many media.

A Model of Brand reveals the intricacy and interrelationships of branding and illuminates the topic in surprising ways. Dubberly's goal in making the poster was to put all the key ideas in one place to make a reference tool, as well as an explanation. Another objective of the model was to show how brand and experience are linked: 'Graphic designers often focus on identity; interface designers tend to focus on interaction; yet these areas overlap quite a lot, for example, in function, look, and feel.'

The horizontal axis leads the eye from left to right, beginning with the brand's 'stewards,' moving to its 'promise,' its 'product,' and then to the user's 'experience.' Dubberly explains: 'Stewards imagine promise, promise guides product, product delivers experience, experience shapes perception, perception builds brand, and brand can be measured by stewards.' This cycle is underscored by

the typography, with the word 'steward' appearing both at the left edge of the map and bleeding off the right, suggesting that the right edge wraps back around to the left—as if the poster were wrapped around a cylinder. One rule that Dubberly insists on following, even though it is difficult, is only using a term once on a map. Each term is clearly defined and supported with examples.

The vertical axis connects the internal meaning of the 'brand' to the external systems that impact upon it, and the two axes intersect where 'experience' meets 'perception.' Dubberly refers to this interlocking structure as an *armature*. This branching architecture is present in all of his maps and provides a continuous flow that visually captures the recursive relationships among the parts that he strives to uncover. Each corner of the poster is filled with further detail: indices, definitions, and principles.

'The whole structure is a space which suggests paths or narratives to explore.'

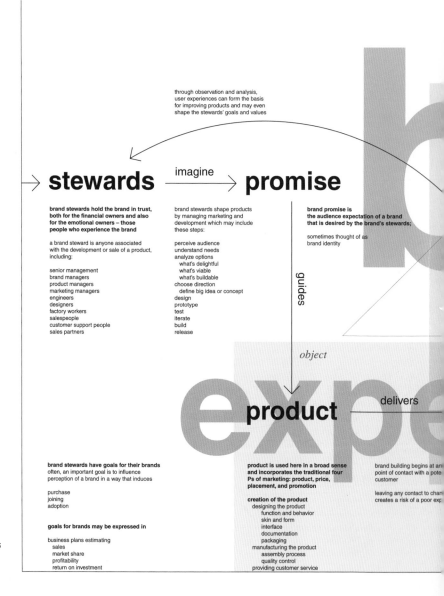

A Model of Brand (detail). The complexity of the map absorbs the viewer in a detailed hierarchy that sparks discovery through a logical sequence of associations.

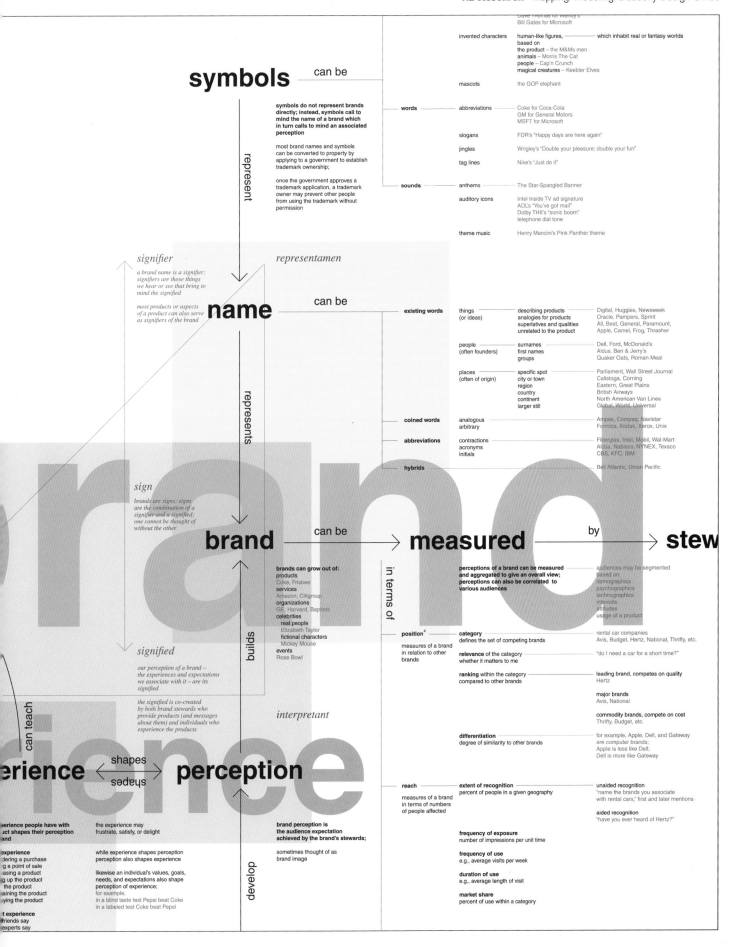

symbols — can be

symbols do not represent brands directly; instead, symbols call to mind the name of a brand which in turn calls to mind an associated perception

most brand names and symbols can be converted to property by applying to a government to establish trademark ownership;

once the government approves a trademark application, a trademark owner may prevent other people from using the trademark without permission

represent

words	invented characters	human-like figures, based on	which inhabit real or fantasy worlds
			Dave Thomas for Wendy's
			Bill Gates for Microsoft
		the product – the M&Ms men	
		animals – Morris The Cat	
		people – Cap'n Crunch	
		magical creatures – Keebler Elves	
	mascots	the GOP elephant	
	abbreviations	Coke for Coca-Cola	
		GM for General Motors	
		MSFT for Microsoft	
	slogans	FDR's "Happy days are here again"	
	jingles	Wrigley's "Double your pleasure; double your fun"	
	tag lines	Nike's "Just do it"	
sounds	anthems	The Star-Spangled Banner	
	auditory icons	Intel Inside TV ad signature	
		AOL's "You've got mail"	
		Dolby THX's "sonic boom"	
		telephone dial tone	
	theme music	Henry Mancini's Pink Panther theme	

signifier   *representamen*

a brand name is a signifier; signifiers are those things we hear or see that bring to mind the signified

most products or aspects of a product can also serve as signifiers of the brand

name — can be

existing words	things (or ideas)	describing products	Digital, Huggies, Newsweek
		analogies for products	Oracle, Pampers, Sprint
		superlatives and qualities	All, Best, General, Paramount,
		unrelated to the product	Apple, Camel, Frog, Thrasher
	people (often founders)	surnames	Dell, Ford, McDonald's
		first names	Aldus, Ben & Jerry's
		groups	Quaker Oats, Roman Meal
	places (often of origin)	specific spot	Parliament, Wall Street Journal
		city or town	Calistoga, Corning
		region	Eastern, Great Plains
		country	British Airways
		continent	North American Van Lines
		larger still	Global, World, Universal
coined words	analogous		Ampex, Compaq, Navistar
	arbitrary		Formica, Kodak, Xerox, Unix
abbreviations	contractions		Fiberglas, Intel, Mobil, Wal-Mart
	acronyms		Alcoa, Nabisco, NYNEX, Texaco
	initials		CBS, KFC, IBM
hybrids			Bell Atlantic, Union Pacific

represents

sign

brands are signs; signs are the combination of a signifier and a signified; one cannot be thought of without the other

brand → can be → measured — by → stew

brands can grow out of:
products
Coke, Frisbee
services
Amazon, Citigroup
organizations
GE, Harvard, Baptists
celebrities
  real people
  Elizabeth Taylor
  fictional characters
  Mickey Mouse
events
Rose Bowl

builds

in terms of

perceptions of a brand can be measured and aggregated to give an overall view; perceptions can also be correlated to various audiences

audiences may be segmented based on:
demographics
psychographics
technographics
interests
attitudes
usage of a product

position[4]
measures of a brand in relation to other brands

category
defines the set of competing brands
  rental car companies
  Avis, Budget, Hertz, National, Thrifty, etc.

relevance of the category
whether it matters to me
  "do I need a car for a short time?"

ranking within the category
compared to other brands
  leading brand, competes on quality
  Hertz

  major brands
  Avis, National

  commodity brands, compete on cost
  Thrifty, Budget, etc.

differentiation
degree of similarity to other brands
  for example, Apple, Dell, and Gateway are computer brands;
  Apple is less like Dell;
  Dell is more like Gateway

reach
measures of a brand in terms of numbers of people affected

extent of recognition
percent of people in a given geography
  unaided recognition
  "name the brands you associate with rental cars," first and later mentions

  aided recognition
  "have you ever heard of Hertz?"

frequency of exposure
number of impressions per unit time

frequency of use
e.g., average visits per week

duration of use
e.g., average length of visit

market share
percent of use within a category

signified

our perception of a brand – the experiences and expectations we associate with it – are its signified

the signified is co-created by both brand stewards who provide products (and messages about them) and individuals who experience the products

interpretant

can teach

erience ← shapes / shapes → perception

...erience people have with ...uct shapes their perception ...and

...experience
...dering a purchase
...g a point of sale
...asing a product
... the product
...aining the product
...ying the product

...t experience
...friends say
...experts say

the experience may frustrate, satisfy, or delight

while experience shapes perception perception also shapes experience

likewise an individual's values, goals, needs, and expectations also shape perception of experience;
for example,
in a blind taste test Pepsi beat Coke
in a labeled test Coke beat Pepsi

brand perception is the audience expectation achieved by the brand's stewards;

sometimes thought of as brand image

developed

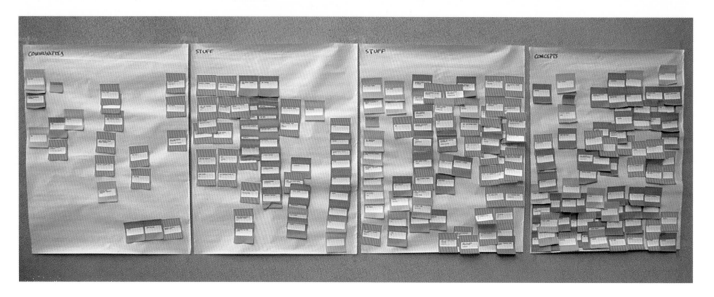

In the first phase of the *Java Technology Concept Map*, every possible term related to Java, found in books and glossaries and cited by users, was written on color-coded sticky notes: components of Java on magenta, organizations involved in the Java community on yellow, Java language terms on green, and general programming terms on orange.

'Design is moving from a world where we were concerned primarily with objects with tangible artifacts to one where increasingly we're concerned with systems and less tangible artifacts. So as designers we have to develop tools for dealing with these intangibles.'

When asked what it was that led him to mapping as a studio focus, Dubberly says, 'Part of it is practical.... Increasingly our practice involves systems or even systems of systems. A system is often a sort of intangible thing— it's hard to see all at once or it has aspects that unfold over time or which might be hidden because they're really small inside a computer or they are just far away.... There are many reasons.' Concept mapping for Dubberly has therefore become an essential tool for defining and detailing the objectives of a project and also for forming a strong partnership with the client.

When DDO was approached to redesign Sun Microsystems' main website for Java developers, they began the design process by diagramming the assignment's context, focusing on the website users' needs and tasks. The *Java Technology Concept Map* became the backbone of an exhaustive process that not only educated the designers about Java, but also aided inclusivity for a large client with a lot of stakeholders in the website design.

DDO began their research by interviewing a series of external developers who used the existing 110,000-page website as well as engineers from Sun. After more than forty interviews, a detailed inventory of the traffic flows on the existing site, and many intense weeks of

work, the team produced a 3 x 15 foot (0.9 x 4.5 meter) diagram with over 400 terms. The first phases were generated with removable sticky notes on foam board to allow the model to be a work in progress. Ongoing reviews and revisions took place over many weeks. Large copies of the map were posted in high-traffic areas inviting reviewers to write revisions on the map and attach sticky notes.

The concept map was most instrumental in the design of the site architecture. The final map (see p. 16) took almost a year to complete. It contains 235 terms, 425 links (relationships), and 110 descriptions. The design of the web pages—their proportions, hierarchy, and typography—were the product of more conventional graphic design practices.

In Dubberly's words, 'Rather than imposing an architecture on the site design, the map informed the site more organically.' Furthermore, when the design team rolled out the mammoth diagram on the conference table they immediately established credibility and facilitated an expanded level of communication with the Sun engineers: 'We immediately had something to talk about and something that piqued their interest....Because of the homework, we were able to have a conversation with them.'

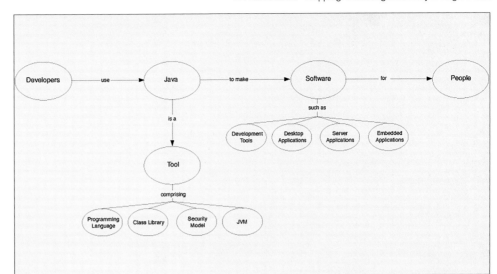

The primary terms for the Java map were identified and configured into a logical armature.

Below: The basic armature remains but more detailed levels of information are woven into the structure.

The final map (see p. 16) was the product of more than 50 interviews, 100 meetings, and 2,000 e-mails.

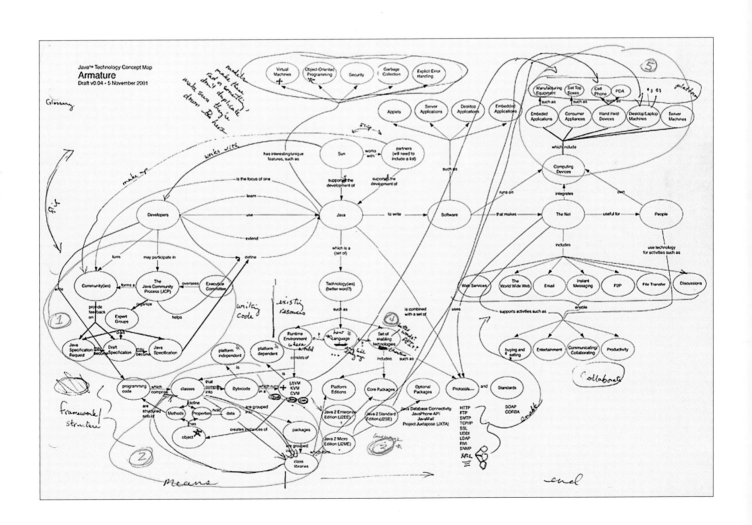

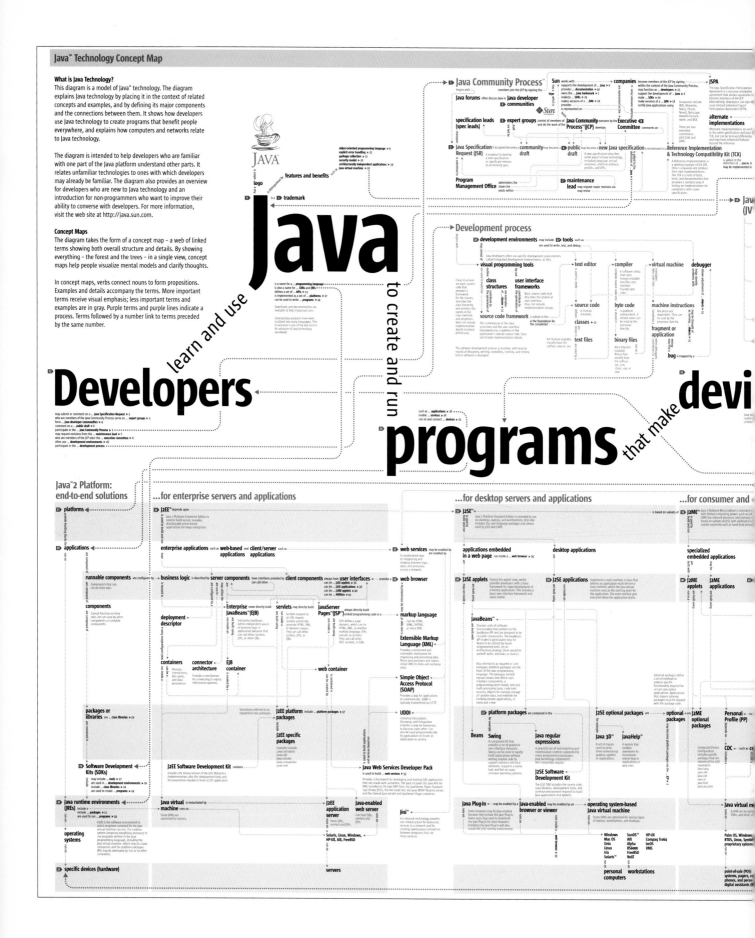

Java™ Technology Concept Map

What is Java Technology?

This diagram is a model of Java™ technology. The diagram explains Java technology by placing it in the context of related concepts and examples, and by defining its major components and the connections between them. It shows how developers use Java technology to create programs that benefit people everywhere, and explains how computers and networks relate to Java technology.

The diagram is intended to help developers who are familiar with one part of the Java platform understand other parts. It relates unfamiliar technologies to ones with which developers may already be familiar. The diagram also provides an overview for developers who are new to Java technology and an introduction for non-programmers who want to improve their ability to converse with developers. For more information, visit the web site at http://java.sun.com.

Concept Maps

The diagram takes the form of a concept map – a web of linked terms showing both overall structure and details. By showing everything – the forest and the trees – in a single view, concept maps help people visualize mental models and clarify thoughts.

In concept maps, verbs connect nouns to form propositions. Examples and details accompany the terms. More important terms receive visual emphasis; less important terms and examples are in gray. Purple terms and purple lines indicate a process. Terms followed by a number link to terms preceded by the same number.

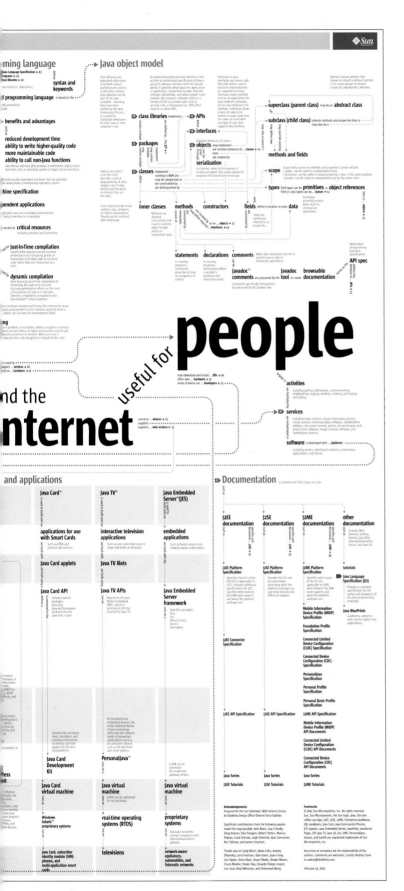

The completed *Java Technology Concept Map*.

Creative DNA
Dubberly Design Office

Hugh Dubberly is a design planner and teacher. The idea of large two-dimensional visual expressions is something he was exposed to from his early childhood. Both of his parents were engineers, and he has fond memories of coloring on the back of large blueprints for electricity-generating stations that his father would bring home.

Dubberly graduated from Rhode Island School of Design with a BFA in graphic design and earned an MFA in graphic design from Yale. At Apple Computer in the late 1980s and early 1990s, Dubberly managed cross-functional design teams and later managed creative services for the entire company. During this time, he also served at the Art Center College of Design in Pasadena as the founding chairman of the computer graphics department.

Intrigued by what the publishing industry would look like on the Internet, he moved on from Apple to become director of interface design for Times Mirror. This led him to Netscape, where, as vice president of design, he managed groups responsible for the design, engineering, and production of Netscape's web portal.

Dubberly founded Dubberly Design Office in 2000. Since then, DDO has helped design software-based products and services for a range of companies, from start-ups to multi-nationals such as Samsung and Johnson & Johnson.

1.3

Johnson Banks

The Client

Crafting distinctive identities for each client has been the focus of Michael Johnson's seven-person practice for over a decade. He founded Johnson Banks twenty years ago, and it took about ten of those years to establish the acclaimed reputation that attracts the variety and caliber of clients they have today. The company's focus is on strategy and the planning portion of projects, and Johnson often spends the first third of an assignment—sometimes as long as six months—looking for 'a gap, or an insight' before beginning the design process. For Johnson this intensive research is what ultimately brings an identity to life and makes it stick, both conceptually and visually. He considers a 'house style' to be completely undesirable: 'If you honestly do what is unique for the client you can't also pass it off as your studio aesthetic.'

'If you honestly do what is unique for the client you can't also pass it off as your studio aesthetic.'

A sampling of some of Johnson Banks's recent identity designs. Each project employs a singular approach fitted to the client and their selected audience.

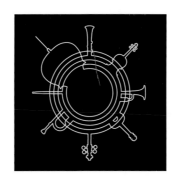

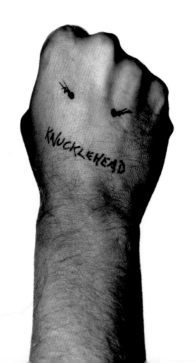

Johnson's fascination with identity design began early on. He acknowledges that he wasn't the stereotypical high school art student 'who hated math, physics, and chemistry.' Nor did he take the traditional foundation course in art that is part of most designers' educations in the UK. Instead, he went straight to university to double major in marketing and visual art. Identity was the subject of his dissertation, and upon graduating he continued to pursue knowledge in that area by taking a job at Wolff Olins, the premier London brand-strategy firm at that time. Johnson explains that it is because of his dual educational background that he can operate comfortably as both the 'suit and the designer—as two people in one, with no translation needed between business-speak and design-speak.' His diverse training also widened his curiosity and his ability to make conceptual connections. He asserts that at the heart of his creative philosophy 'is a nonjudgmental openness to art in all of its forms, coupled with an awareness of where it can live in the world.'

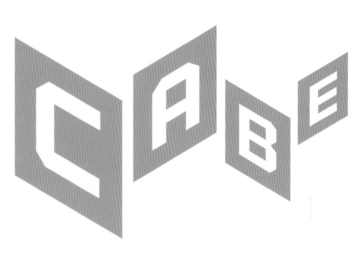

LANDFLEX

Johnson's fluency in both form and function is evident in an identity scheme that the studio recently completed for the Pew Center for Arts & Heritage in Philadelphia. The Pew Center approached him in 2008 with the challenge of designing a unified identity for their multifaceted organization. Instead of seeing this complexity as a burden, Johnson recognized the potential in the organization's multiplicity and harnessed it as the core concept for the identity. His understanding of the component parts of the institution and how they fit together led him to a new model—one that not only clarified the organizational hierarchy but also revealed its flexibility. The result was an elegant modular composition where letters are punched out of solid color blocks and transparently stacked. The logo comes in three different forms, each incorporating the center's seven different divisions. Each division also has its own sub-identity.

'We started thinking of the center and its constituent parts a little like "cards" that we could shuffle and reorganize. The part you wanted to represent was the one on top, but crucially, we allowed glimpses of the other initiatives to peek out behind the main card.'

Johnson Banks's identity for the Pew Center extends across both print and online materials, with sub-identities for each of the center's seven divisions. Online, the logo is animated, further extending the core concept of malleability.

Below: Concept sketches for the logo and online animation.

'The system is set up for a "mother ship with children," but sometimes the children need to become more important.'

Even though Johnson embraces large-scale projects and big-picture planning, he still makes time for hands-on designing. He explains that he has no fixed method but might start with 'process A, and if that doesn't work, move on to B, and so on.' His Think London identity is an example of how one operation can set his process in motion. He says that it was his frustration from trying to completely symbolize 'London' that started a chain of events leading to a unique 'multi-logo' highlighting London as a destination for companies looking to move their business overseas. He began by making a composition out of silhouettes of London landmarks, but when he realized he was building what he described as 'an obvious cliché,' he was so discouraged that he turned the skyline upside down and began adding random elements on top of it. The resulting reflection of unexpected elements immediately revealed its potential for a syntactic pairing of symbolic ideas across the horizon line.

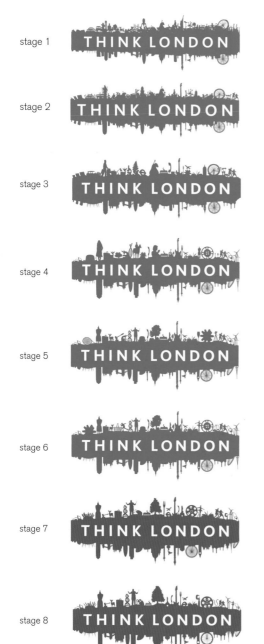

On the Think London website, the identity was made to extend right across the screen so that it also incorporated the menu bar.

Left: These development sketches show the incremental stages of refinement made to complete the logo.

The animated Think London identity comes alive with small movements—DNA twirls, a conductor waves his arms, a movie reel rotates, a page of a book turns, and an airplane soars in the distance—all combining to demonstrate what London has to offer to a company looking to move its business there.

'The reflection is the real skyline. The new skyline contains everything from music to parks, soccer, ballerinas, DNA spirals, and micrometers.'

Johnson values drawing as part of the design process because of its capacity for testing concepts and 'avoiding unnecessary time spent making detailed mock-ups of fruitless ideas.' He has also always been a proponent of high technology; shortly after he started working in the professional world in the late 1980s, he orchestrated a contest at his then employers between the computer department and the art department to prove that the former was more efficient. He embraces digital media and its potential to animate the identities he creates and further extend their personalities. In the case of Think London, the toylike parts make subtle movements, and the logo almost seems to breathe.

Each application is an opportunity to see the logo live in a different way. Here the designer takes advantage of the horizontal span of a printed brochure in accordion format.

Another project, a complete redesign of the identity campaign for Anthony Nolan, a London charity that recruits donors to sign up on a blood stem cell register, illustrates a synthesis of the client's mission and contemporary graphic design.

The directive for the new identity was to generate awareness and attract new donors, especially from a younger,

male audience. As a new name for the organization was not being considered for historical reasons, a graphic solution was needed. The directness of the typography sets up a tangible sense of purpose and a call to action: by linking the matching letters across the logotype, it becomes a direct illustration of the way that a donor can 'be a match and save a life.' This principle is carried across into print and the web.

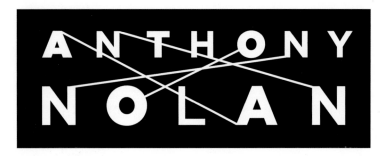

BE A MATCH, SAVE A LIFE

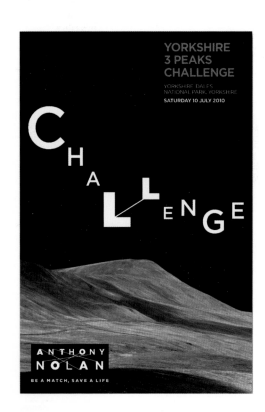

An embedded chance operation both establishes the typography and reflects the action of finding a match in this playful design for a serious mission—increasing blood stem cell donations for life-saving transplants—that was aimed at young audiences. The logo's bold typography sets up a cohesive yet changeable identity adapted to posters and ads for charity-sponsored events.

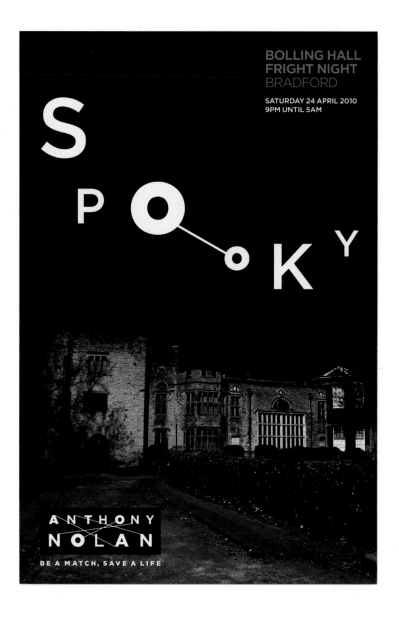

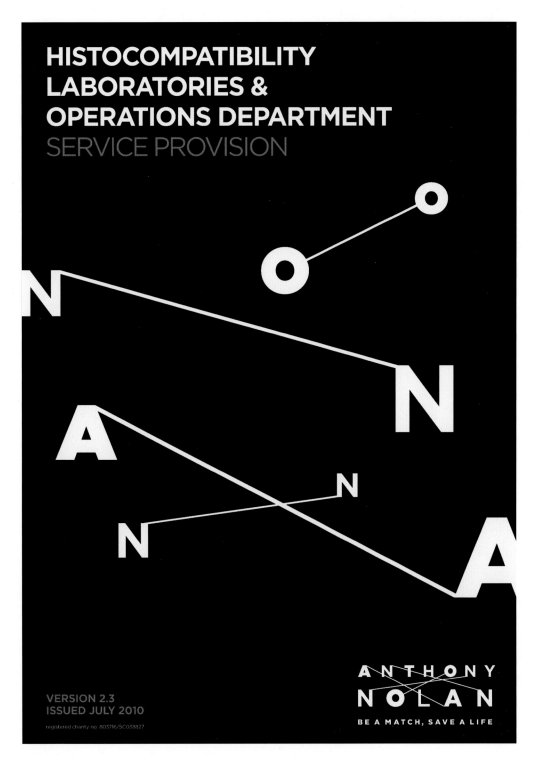

HISTOCOMPATIBILITY
LABORATORIES &
OPERATIONS DEPARTMENT
SERVICE PROVISION

VERSION 2.3
ISSUED JULY 2010
registered charity no. 803716/SC038827

ANTHONY
NOLAN
BE A MATCH, SAVE A LIFE

Creative DNA
Johnson Banks

Michael Johnson is the creative director of the internationally renowned design company Johnson Banks. The company works predominately in the cultural, ethical, government, and charity sectors, and has produced brand and identity schemes for the British Government, CABE, Shelter, Christian Aid, Save the Children, and the British Film Institute.

Johnson has always been equally interested in art and business, appreciating a wide range of visual approaches. He remembers being inspired as a student by books as diverse as *Meggs' History of Graphic Design*, Herbert Spencer's *Pioneers of Modern Typography*, and Milton Glaser's first book. These influences yielded some unusual early student work, including 'rendering something in Push-Pin-like pastels and then strangely anchoring it on a square, reminiscent of Piet Zwart.'

Johnson is the author of *Problem Solved*, a primer on design and communication.

inspiration.

2 Inspiration

In his book *Designerly Ways of Knowing,* Nigel Cross quotes S. A. Gregory: 'The scientific method is a pattern of problem-solving behavior employed in finding out the nature of what exists, whereas the design method is a pattern of behavior employed in inventing things of value which do not yet exist. Science is analytic; design is constructive.' Gregory's eloquent contrast of the scientific and design methods of working positions the designer as one who explores in order to originate. This chapter, 'Inspiration,' examines the forces that initiate exploration and spark discovery.

For the designer, inspiration is always present, even before a specific assignment begins. It can be sustained through life-long interests or triggered by small, everyday events. Curiosity also plays a critical role, and designers who learn to ask questions develop an openness that maintains their creative momentum.

Inspiration can have a precise origin or be prompted by an ambient stimulus that enters the consciousness through the senses. It can be sparked by divergent visual forms from other disciplines, built on recurring conceptual interests, or even arrived at through a series of chance operations.

The case studies that follow are focused on how inspiration comes into play in the graphic design process: 'Found Objects' shows how, in a state of heightened receptivity, designers Melle Hammer and Yara Khoury discovered an Arabic alphabet in a nest of tagliatelle; 'Materials' explores how Graphic Thought Facility's pursuit of unexpected materials constantly fuels their imagination; 'Collage' details the give and take of collage art that informs the work of Skolos Wedell; and 'Synaesthesia' examines the work of James Goggin, whose obsession with senses and common sense invigorates his process.

Melle Hammer and Yara Khoury

Found Objects

For Dutch designer Melle Hammer, imagination is a way of life, and life is a continuous adventure in creativity; inspiration is everywhere, and ingenuity can be sparked by frustration, curiosity, or just plain fun.

Recently Hammer was paired with Lebanese type designer Yara Khoury as part of the 'Typographic Matchmaking in the City' project, commissioned by the Khatt Foundation, a Netherlands-based organization dedicated to advancing Arabic typography and design research. Hammer and Khoury were one of five teams of Dutch and Arab designers whose assignment was to design three-dimensional bilingual typefaces for use at large scale in public spaces and for architectural applications. Khoury was selected because of her expertise as a type designer and Hammer because of his experimental approach to design problem solving.

Learning the distinct characteristics and idiosyncrasies of Arabic writing was a fascinating experience for Hammer: 'In Arabic, they don't have upper and lower case. The design of each letterform depends on the position of the letter in the word, and for almost all of these there are at least four designs: one where it's at the beginning of a word, one where it's in the middle, one where it's at the end, and one where it stands alone! This variation is necessary because of the way Arabic letters stream together to make up a word in one continuous form, similar to cursive writing.

'I bought myself a nest of dried tagliatelle. I broke it apart, and spread it on the table. I said, "If my observation is right, then this must contain your alphabet."... And yes, her alphabet was almost there.'

A broken nest of tagliatelle inspired Hammer and Khoury's three-dimensional typeface.

Facing page: Letters are fabricated using a three-dimensional printer that outputs objects from digital files by building up successive layers of thin plastic strands.

There are twenty-eight consonants and all but six take four varied shapes, with those six taking only the stand-alone shape and the end shape. Hammer explains, 'They are the same letterform but they all look different.' There are two types of vowels in Arabic: long and short. Long vowels exist as letterforms, but short vowels are indicated among the consonants with smaller diacritical marks added to the letters and are used primarily in religious texts, scholarly writing, and poetry.

After spending a day with Khoury and feeling a bit overwhelmed by all the samples of Arabic writing he had seen, Hammer joked that the letters looked like a plate of tagliatelle. To prove his point, he bought a nest of tagliatelle at the supermarket, brought it to Khoury, and mischievously broke it and spread it out on the table. Within the collection of noodle fragments Khoury was indeed able to identify almost the entire alphabet.

Hammer became aquainted with the ribbonlike forms of Arabic calligraphy as Khoury drew various words for him during their first meeting. Below is Khoury's drawing of the word 'bridge.'

This playful exercise was the beginning of their Kasheeda typeface, a three-dimensional banner alphabet that consists of ribbon-shaped letterforms and is available in both Arabic and Latin. Its lyrical forms are legible at one exact viewing angle. The typeface is intended exclusively for use in three-dimensional space and can be made as small as a jewel or as large as 20 feet (6 meters) high—large enough to have a word cover a building facade.

Initial letterform prototypes were made from thin strips of metal bent into shape; for the final production, however, bending was too hard to calibrate. Casting was considered but was too costly. Finally, three-dimensional rapid printing proved to be the best option. In this process, an object is made by layering thin strands of plastic material, and multiple compound shapes can be generated efficiently from computer files. Reaching the production stage of the project took a year of drawing and back-and-forth that Hammer describes as a 'dense dialogue with the material and the circumstances that led to the final product.'

'We defined the curves of the letters with our hands; we didn't make any drawings.'

Above and left: Yara Khoury working on elaborate prototypes made from hand-folded ribbons of thin sheet metal.

Matching Latin and Arabic alphabets were both inspired by the characteristic bends of the pasta fragments.

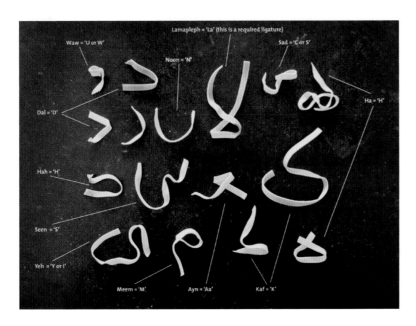

The designers' analysis of the pasta, identifying Arabic letterforms. Khoury was able to find almost every Arabic character in Hammer's broken nest of tagliatelle.

'Arabic has unusual qualities that you could write a thick book about. It's eye-opening and fascinating.'

Prototype letterforms were carefully organized by Khoury, with specifications for baseline, height, and dimensions.

The metal forms were translated into final drawings and programmed by an experienced technician for output on a three-dimensional printer.

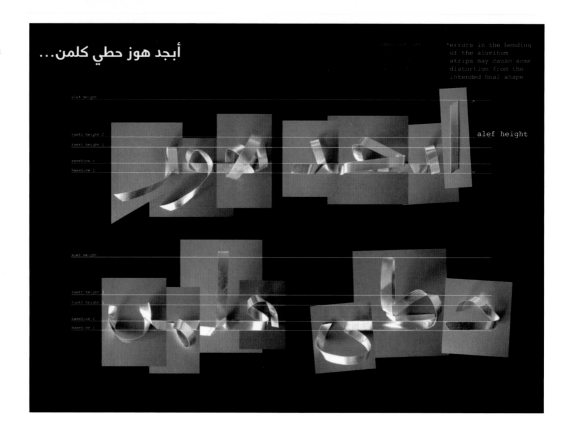

أبجد هوز حطي كلمن...

*errors in the bending of the aluminum strips may cause some distortion from the intended final shape

alef height

alef height

'It was the material demanding—telling us what is possible and what is not; and it was the software demanding—telling us what is possible and what is not.'

The metal prototypes were meticulously cataloged and carefully labeled.

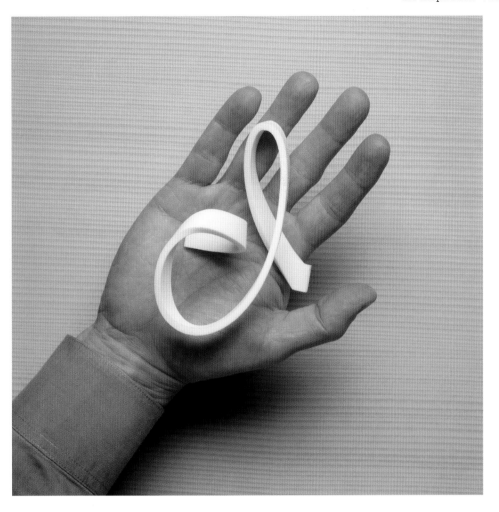

Above: Individual letter *d* in the Kasheeda typeface. Letters (both Arabic and Latin) are fabricated individually and designed to be clicked together to form continuous words on a sloping baseline.

Below: Words are entered into an online interface before being output by a three-dimensional printer. The connections between the letters are simulated onscreen.

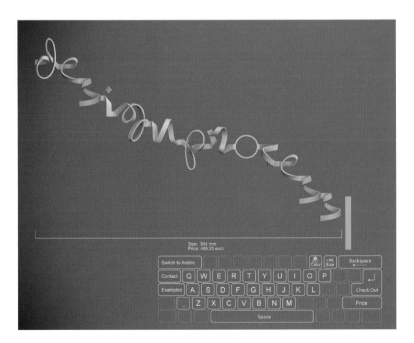

Creative DNA
Melle Hammer
Yara Khoury

Melle Hammer began his career as a graphic designer in an advertising agency at the age of eighteen, just before he graduated from Gerrit Rietveld Academie, Amsterdam. Since then, his output has included graphic design, furniture, industrial products, and stage sets. He has also worked on film and theater projects, producing the title sequence for Johan van der Keuken's 1996 film *Amsterdam Global Village*, and collaborating with Jaap Blonk on an experimental theater piece for voice and typography.

Hammer has taught typography at Gerrit Rietveld Academie, and was chair of the design department at Jan van Eyck Academie in Maastricht from 1999 through 2001. He has lectured and led workshops in both Europe and the US. He is cofounder and current organizer of DesignInquiry, a nonprofit educational venture that brings together designers from different fields to generate new work and ideas around a single topic.

Yara Khoury is an award-winning type and book designer who lives and works in Lebanon. She received a BA in Graphic Design from Notre Dame University, Lebanon, and an MA in Art and Design with distinction from Middlesex University, London.

Khoury is currently Design Director at Al Mohtaraf Design House, in Bierut, one of the most prominent design firms in the Arab world. She has been responsible for the design of major corporate identities, corporate publications, books, magazines and Arabic typefaces. Khoury teaches graphic design at Notre Dame University and Lebanese American University in Lebanon.

2.2

Materials

'We were looking to break out of what we perceived as elaborate form for the sake of form and saw materials as a way to express meaning with more directness and honesty.'

Graphic Thought Facility, jointly owned by Paul Neale, Huw Morgan, and Andrew Stevens, is a London-based group of graphic designers who think, meticulously, in every sense of the word: reason, imagination, intention, and recollection are all central to their process. Their balance of research and contemplation results in a gentle persuasiveness that is evident as Stevens describes the way the studio likes to work: 'You find the creative space in a project—between all of the pragmatic restrictions and the desires of a client. You try to find that little space to work in.'

Beginning with pragmatics is fundamental to GTF's creative process, accommodating restrictions as well as setting up systems to support them. They are rarely involved with self-initiated projects or 'leisure graphics just for themselves' and prefer to set their ideas in motion within the constraints of a real commercial context. They maintain a backlog of concepts and processes that can be applied when the right project comes along, and they are always asking practical questions: What's the budget? How quickly does the project or object need to be made and distributed? How long does it have to last? In this way, GTF consider themselves to operate in more of a commonsense way than a strategic one. There is never a polarity between business and creativity in their design practice because they see the client as someone who can help in the conversation and who shares an accordant attitude and vision.

One of the most striking things about GTF's work is the innovative and often unconventional materials that they use to reveal the essence of the subject at hand: cocoa powder for a café logo, doorway lettering for a small Soho-based production company, and mull—usually a hidden part of bookbinding—overlaying the cover of a Tord Boontje monograph. Even though the effects generated by the materials are often subliminal and by no means the primary vehicle of communication, they set up an atmosphere that makes the work seem 'right.'

This insight into the power of materials began when Stevens and Neale were students at the Royal College of Art in London and discovered the materials collection housed in the main library there. The collection was set up primarily for interior- and product-design majors but, as Stevens recalls, 'we wandered in there as graphic designers and we'd never seen this stuff....There were these incredible materials and processes that had very evocative associations.' Neale would collect manufacturers' phone numbers from the resources library and come to the college early in the morning, half an hour before the secretary arrived, so he could use the office phone to order samples.[1]

Their attraction to materiality and low-tech processes was a reaction against the computer-focused, highly embellished two-dimensional work that had gone on just prior to their time at the RCA. They were looking to break out of what they perceived as elaborate 'form for the sake of form' and saw the inventive use of materials as a way to express meaning with directness and honesty.

Even today, their work is focused within the realm of the physical object. 'Ultimately, nearly all the graphics we do are 3-D,' says Stevens. Even in a more prescribed format like book design, the qualities of a book as an object are reinforced: 'the weight of the cover, the weight of the paper, and how it's bound.'

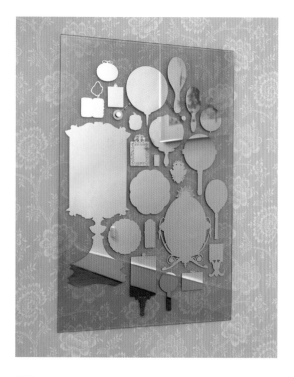

GTF's *Mirror Mirror*, designed for the Victoria & Albert Museum, was inspired by the museum's collection of Victorian hand mirrors.

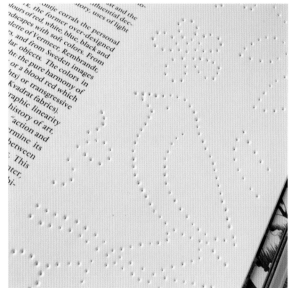

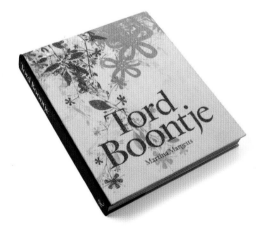

Mighty Productions identity design, inspired by 'Soho doorway' lettering.

Identity design for Marks & Spencer's Café Revive, made with cocoa powder and stencils.

GTF's large-format monograph on product designer Tord Boontje is covered in mull, a material that is normally a hidden structural component in the bookbinding process.

A pattern of holes, inspired by a technique that Boontje developed to perforate molten glass, decorates the large white margins of the interior pages.

GTF enjoy exhibition design because it provides opportunities to push the potential of materials and fabrication even further, and it puts them in contact with specialists in areas like architecture, lighting, multimedia, and furniture design. Their comprehensive design program for the 54th Carnegie International—a survey of contemporary American art that dates back to 1896 and takes place every four years—shows how a gesture that begins with one physical material can be scaled to fill several roles.

The signature motif was inspired by the ribbon attached to the Carnegie Prize medal awarded at the exhibition, directly linked to the concept of recognition. The designers were intrigued by the ribbon's potential to be both old and new, formal and informal—evoking both the tradition of the Carnegie International and the contemporary quality of the art it presents. In relation to the medal, the ribbon had historic connotations, but as a graphic element it was expressive and flexible. As Stevens notes, 'It allowed us to turn the volume of the identity up and down as we wanted.' It could be presented in a more fixed linear black-and-white graphic version or applied to any surface in a more organic, colorful, and playful gesture. The ribbons were trailed along walls and floors to function as a loosely structured signage system that guided people through the massive exhibition. The cloth-bound exhibition catalog, also designed by GTF, carried the ribbon motif on its cover and also as a literal object within it, in the form of a bookmark. This homogeneity between celebration and commemoration further underscored the exhibition's contemporary and traditional associations.

Left and facing page, top:
The flexibility of GTF's graphic ribbons allowed them to serve both decorative and directional functions within the space.

Exhibition design: Michael Maltzen Architecture.

CARNEGIE INTERNATIONAL
2004–5
9 OCTOBER 2004–20 MARCH 2005

The ribbon held up equally well as a simple, flat black-and-white translation.

'Ultimately nearly all the graphics we do are 3-D....If it's a book, you pick it up and it's the weight of the cover, the weight of the paper, and how it's bound.'

The ribbon also appeared as a bookmark in the 54th Carnegie International catalog, designed by GTF.

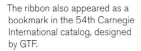

The Carnegie Prize medal, which is engraved on the title page of the catalog, was the original inspiration for GTF's ribbon theme.

Recently GTF had an unusual opportunity to see how their process has evolved when they were asked to redo the *Who Am I?* exhibition gallery for the Science Museum in London. True to its title, the multifaceted exhibition explores the many forces—both environmental and genetic—that make us who we are. The first design was commissioned in 2000, and the update was finished in 2010. Comparing the two versions is a fascinating case study in how materials can be used to reflect content over time.

The extremely popular gallery was in need of an upgrade due to general wear and tear, but more critically to incorporate ten years of advances in the science of biogenetics. Stevens explains, 'There was a new story to tell as well as the desire to make it look fresher and up to date.' The Science Museum assembled the original team of curators, architects, and media designers to undertake the redo. 'It worked well because we understood the problems and had a lot of affection for the project,' says

Stevens. While the content had evolved, many of the general challenges for conveying the content remained: the need to create impact and hierarchy as well as incorporate a degree of flexibility, to design 'things that look permanent but systems that can accommodate updates, change, corrections, and new objects.'

The original 2000 exhibition employed a battery of what were then cutting-edge, high-tech materials and processes, introduced by a large electronic 'caterpillar' in the entryway. The display components, including object numbers and label plates, had been cut from photoetched sheets of metal. The components were designed to be adapted to different configurations using fold-out stands and feet, in order to accommodate a variety of viewing angles: from the floor, at case height, or on the wall. Flexibility was a critical part of the original brief, so the label plates had also been designed with stamped tabs to hold laser printouts that could be easily edited and updated as information changed.

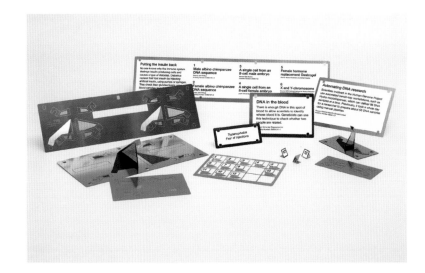

'It's nice because, as a graphic designer, you can be acceptably naive about fabrication methods and you can turn standard processes on their head—you can do something the "wrong way" and make something right.'

The 2000 *Who Am I?* exhibition at London's Science Museum required a flexible system of object display labels that could accommodate a variety of viewing angles.

GTF designed a system of components, made from photoetched steel plates, that could be adapted to different configurations using fold-out tabs and feet.

Overall exhibition design: Casson Mann.

'So often we're building an underlying, supporting part of the text, rather than the main story itself. We're finding ways of communicating the text that encompass all the things we talked about. Is it durable? Is it flexible? Is it affordable? And then, after all that, does it feel right? Does it help the experience feel appropriate?'

To reflect the shift in science over the past decade, the *Who Am I?* exhibition was redesigned in 2010, using a more ethereal design vocabulary. Delicate materials and ambient interactive projections provided a softer interpretation of the human being in a more biologically based atmosphere. GTF sensed that the technologies had moved on, and they looked in particular at materials that might be inserted into human bodies, such as joint replacements and breast implants. This led them to explore the possibilities of using silicon to reflect a more organic way of thinking about technology.

The static cases that had occupied the central spine of the gallery in the original exhibition were replaced with a fluid, interactive interface designed by the company AllofUs. People attending the exhibition are filmed at the entrance and 'encoded' in a series of dots that are then projected as an avatar on the back wall of the gallery. In

Why do you look like that?

Your features, your physique and your colouring were mainly decided in your mother's womb. Your fetal development was subtly orchestrated by a set of genes that you share with mice, butterflies and even worms. But genes weren't the only factor – your environment also shaped the way you look.

GTF updated the aesthetic of the 2010 exhibition with object numbers and labels in molded soft silicon materials.

Overall exhibition design: Casson Mann.

Interactive design: AllofUs.

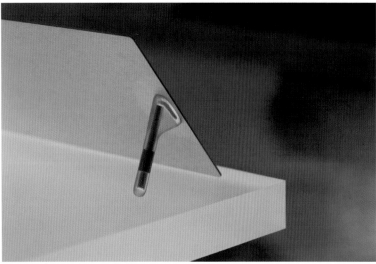

Silicon materials were meticulously detailed and molded to support object labels.

Stevens's view, the arrival of this new type of interaction has created opportunities for more open, unified exhibition spaces. 'There's maybe less variation of graphic languages but there is just as much experimentation, and it's more focused.'

Label plates, a critical part of the display, changed dramatically in the 2010 redesign: the photoetched steel of 2000 was replaced with flexible, molded silicon. Stevens reflects, 'Both materials did the job equally well and it was just a shift of aesthetic.'

For both the 2000 and 2010 galleries, GTF pursued a system and vocabulary of materials that reflected the content of the exhibition and its time frame from both a practical and expressive point of view. The two exhibitions illustrate GTF's attention to materials and the inspiration they always find in them.

Creative DNA
Graphic Thought Facility

Paul Neale, Andrew Stevens, and Nigel Robinson founded Graphic Thought Facility (GTF) in 1990. The three had shared a space during their master's program at the Royal College of Art in London. GTF is currently jointly owned by three directors: Paul Neale, Andrew Stevens, and Huw Morgan.

Working predominantly for cultural and retail clients, GTF have created identities for London's Design Museum and Frieze Art Fair, and home-furnishings retailer Habitat, among others. They are also known for their exhibition graphics for national and international museums and galleries.

In 2006 a retrospective of GTF's work was exhibited at DDD Gallery in Osaka, Japan. In 2008 GTF were the subject of the Art Institute of Chicago's first exhibition devoted solely to graphic design—*Graphic Thought Facility: Resourceful Design*, a survey of GTF projects from the last ten years.

GTF have lectured widely on graphic design at institutions including Ecole cantonale d'art de Lausanne (ECAL), Switzerland; Jan van Eyck Academie, Maastricht; Fabrica, Treviso; California Institute of the Arts (CalArts); Walker Arts Center, Minneapolis; and many UK colleges.

In contrast with the crisp, bent aluminum in the design of the 2000 exhibition, the new label plates floated on organic flexible silicon brackets.

Object numbers were screened onto silicon surfaces.

1. John L. Walters and Nick Bell, 'Reputations: Graphic Thought Facility,' *Eye* no. 39, vol. 10, Spring 2001.

2.3

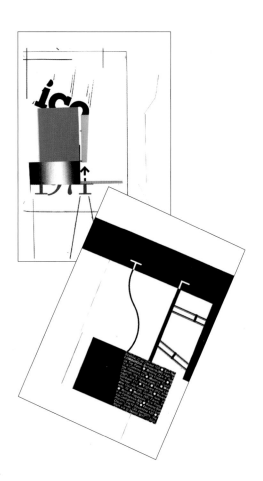

'Once a project is underway in our studio, more often than not, the discarded scraps at the edge of the desktop are far more provocative than the project being "designed."'

Skolos Wedell

Collage

The creative act of collage can provide endless inspiration for graphic designers. Everything in a designer's vocabulary—words, ephemera, materials, colors, and contexts—can be recombined to create unique visual and verbal phenomena. These unexpected formal arrangements engage both our minds and our eyes, and challenge our preconceptions.

For Nancy Skolos and Thomas Wedell, collage is a fruitful starting point for many projects. This interest in letting go of a deliberate process originated in the early stages of their careers, while working with paste-ups: the scraps at the edge of the drawing board and layers of cut-up color paper in flat file drawers proved more provocative than the projects being 'designed.' Gradually this led to an open-mindedness that extended into every phase of their process and provided flexibility in mixing type and image, form and concept.

At the start of a project, Skolos and Wedell often begin by looking through sketchbooks filled with a backlog of collages to see if there are any that might fit with the subject at hand. For them, form is a primary concern, and collage provides a means to simultaneously consider the impact of compositional moves while also brainstorming a concept. The fluidity of collage assists in the formal configuration of a subject and also sparks symbolic associations, not privileging one over the other but allowing both to grow in tandom.

For their 2010 poster for the Lyceum Traveling Fellowship in Architecture, Skolos and Wedell drew inspiration from cultural influences and folded them into a collage process to create a symbolic image for the fellowship's annual student competition. Each year the Lyceum Fellowship committee invites selected schools of architecture to participate in a competition based on a program written by a high-profile practicing architect. While the winning proposals are not intended for actual construction, the students are challenged to meet all of the program's specifications. The poster for this event is printed in a limited edition as well as distributed to the participants online. It is intended to provide an 'atmosphere' or attitude for the assignment, not to suggest a solution or hint at what the judges may be looking for in the final entries. The 2010 program, written by Steven Ehrlich, centered on designing an International Community Center for Abuja, the capital city of Nigeria.

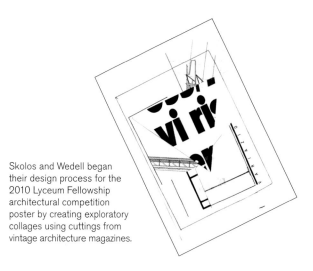

Skolos and Wedell began their design process for the 2010 Lyceum Fellowship architectural competition poster by creating exploratory collages using cuttings from vintage architecture magazines.

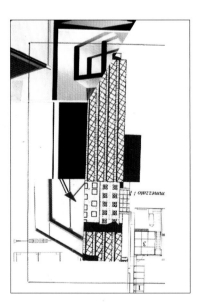
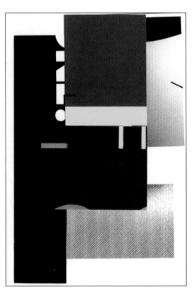
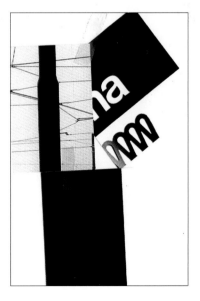

Some of the original collage
sketches that inspired the
final design for the poster.

Excited about the visual richness of Nigerian culture, the designers set out to tie it to the theme of architecture by constructing an African mask as the central image for the poster. The first step was to look through their archive of collage sketches for compositions that implied a structure for a face. There wasn't one perfect design that stood out so they combined pieces of many collage sketches into one.

In order to make the mask design more architectural, they began to translate the collages into an object. Wedell constructed a series of small-scale paper models, mixing geometric elements from the collages with specific forms from the Nigerian masks. This step was critical and helped the designers define the intersection between the African masks and the abstracted architecture represented in the paper collage.

Low-resolution photographs were taken of the paper mock-ups to test camera angles and lighting possibilities. Using Adobe Photoshop, Skolos superimposed additional collage elements over these images in order to see how the architectural theme and mask were coming together and to suggest possibilities for typographic explorations. The discoveries sparked by the initial collage process continued as each stage of the project unfolded, with an attitude of give and take that allowed 'mistakes' and unexpected juxtapositions to disclose better results.

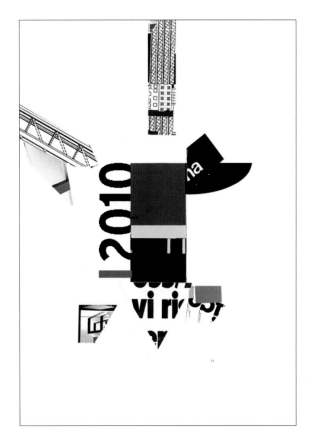

Inspired by the Lyceum competition's focus on Nigeria, Skolos and Wedell decided to incorporate an African mask into their poster design. Individual collage sketches were scanned and reconfigured in Photoshop to create a more symmetrical mask-like image.

Small paper models were constructed in order to test assumptions about the final mask construction—the centerpiece of the overall poster composition.

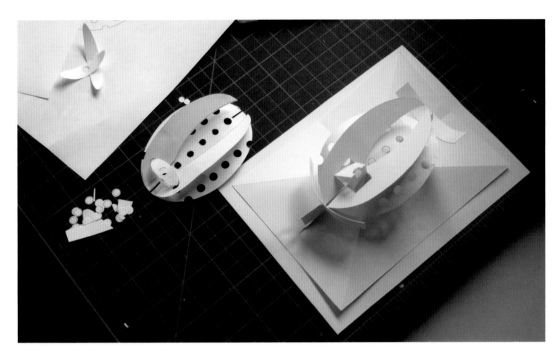

A final paper model was made from a print of the detailed working drawings. At this stage, final adjustments were made to the drawings and a set of laser-cut acrylic parts were produced.

The final paper model was also used to explore lighting possibilities and determine the overall poster composition.

The collage sketch was layered over a test image in Photoshop to try out different graphic and typographic elements.

Once the paper model was finalized, full-scale part drawings were completed in Adobe Illustrator. The pieces were then laser-cut from Plexiglas, and some were heat-formed to match the contours of the smaller paper structure. The final model was finished in paint and then covered in textured papers. A faceted base was assembled from triangular sections of foam board, which was also covered in wood-grain paper. This supported and framed the mask and served as the background for the entire poster composition.

The designing and building of the model was only the initial step in the creation of the poster; the next stage was photographing the final assembly. The model was placed on a low platform and positioned directly beneath the camera. A combination of spotlighting for drama and large diffused sources for overall fill were used to light the model.

During the photographic session, it was very important that the relationship between the camera and subject not be disturbed once the final composition had been determined. For this reason the camera was tethered directly to the computer, enabling minute lighting changes and multiple exposures to be made without touching either the model or the camera.

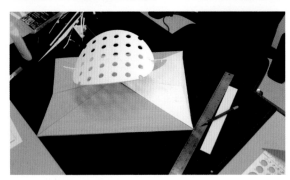

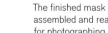

Top: Selected components of the acrylic mask were heated in an oven and molded around existing curved objects—in this example, a wastebasket.

Middle: Precut base sections were cleaned and covered with a wood-grain paper.

Bottom: The finished contoured components are assembled on the base.

The finished mask assembled and ready for photographing.

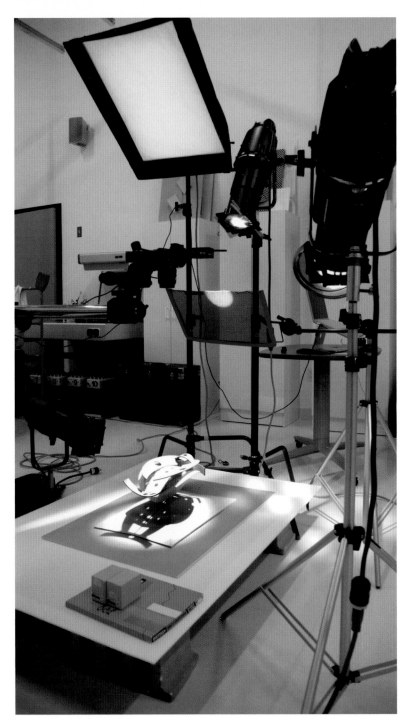

The finished mask was placed below the camera and illuminated with a combination of spotlights and large diffused light boxes.

With the camera tethered to the computer, it was possible to make subtle lighting adjustments without disturbing the position of the camera or the mask.

'The photographic phase of the project brought the object to life with light and synthesized it back into a cohesive two-dimensional form.'

Once the final exposure was achieved, additional work to the mask image was completed in Photoshop in order to further transform the model from a physical object to a graphic form. Once the mask was incorporated into the poster, a number of variations in overall color, contrast, and typographic configuration were tried. Finally, a combination of inverting the original image, masking, and digitally manipulating specific areas provided the graphic quality Skolos and Wedell were looking for—a fusion of type and image.

'An open process, sparked by collage, leads to a seemingly endless feedback loop of possibilities.'

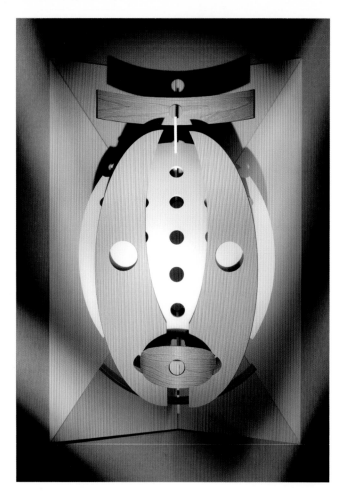

The final photograph of the mask, ready to be incorporated into the poster image.

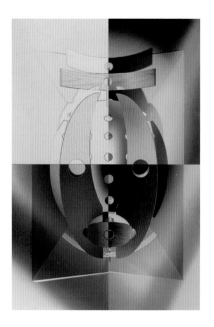

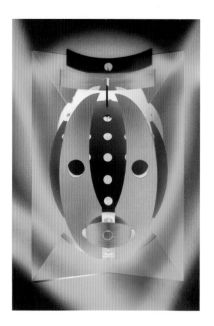

The final poster image was arrived at through a series of experiments with digital transformations.

Once the image was resolved, a number of typographic configurations were explored. The desire to enhance the graphic qualities of the original Nigerian mask was key in arranging the typography.

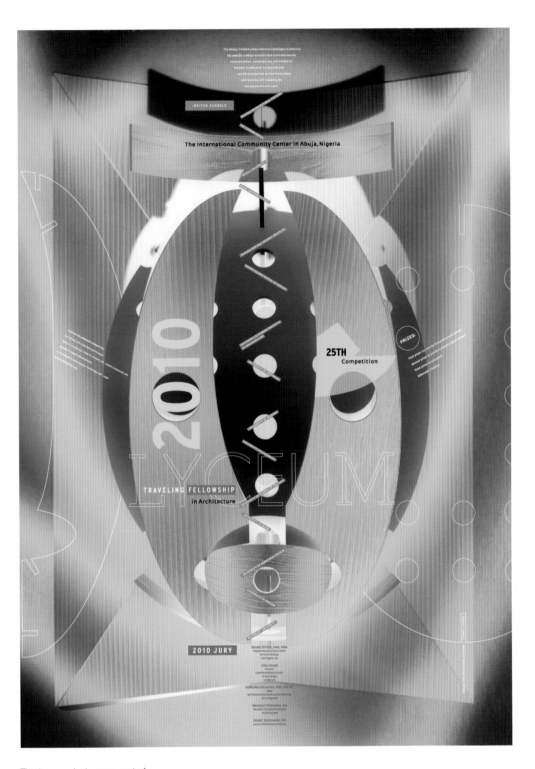

The typography became part of
the image, with the poster text
forming a central zigzag that
echoed the designs of the mask.
The *0* in the date positioned
itself as the eye in the mask.

Creative DNA
Skolos Wedell

Nancy Skolos and Thomas
Wedell grew up in the midwest
United States—Skolos in Ohio
and Wedell in Michigan. Skolos's
father was a commercial artist
and her mother a music teacher.
Skolos is an amateur clarinetist
and considers music to be an
important influence on her work.
Wedell's parents were both
elementary school teachers and
his father introduced him to a
life-long appreciation of film that
informs his understanding of
photography and storytelling.

The two met as students at
Cranbrook Academy of Art in
the mid-1970s and established
a studio in Boston in the 1980s.
They have always been interested
in exploring the boundaries
between graphic design and
photography, creating collaged
three-dimensional photographic
images influenced by modern
painting, technology, and architecture. With a home and studio
halfway between Boston and
Providence, they balance their
commitments to professional
practice and teaching at the
Rhode Island School of Design.

The studio's work has been
widely published and exhibited,
and has received numerous
awards, including a second
prize in the 2011 Lahti Poster
Biennial and a gold medal in
the 2010 International Poster
Biennale, Warsaw. Skolos
Wedell's posters are included in
the graphic design collections of
the Metropolitan Museum of Art
and the Museum of Modern Art,
New York; the Israel Museum,
Jerusalem; and the Museum
für Gestaltung, Zurich. In 2006
they coauthored the book *Type,
Image, Message*.

Skolos is an elected member
of the Alliance Graphique
Internationale and a Boston
AIGA Fellow.

James Goggin

Synaesthesia

'I wish I were a synaesthete,' proclaims James Goggin, founder of the graphic design studio Practise, as he reflects on his creative process. Though Goggin says this somewhat in jest, the comment reveals the unique way he draws upon and mixes sensory experiences to evoke resonance in his design work.

There is a directness in Goggin's work. Deceptively minimalist on the surface, his designs trigger sound, touch, and memory. Color is often key in forging this sensory connection with the viewer.

'Most of my color choices involve me deliberately trying to not pick a color.'

Color has always been an area of keen interest for Goggin—one that he researches avidly and often uses in his own writing, lecturing, and teaching. His interest in color runs parallel to his commitment to straightforwardness in communication. He explains, 'I'm always trying to establish a system where the logic of the project dictates the color rather than any kind of decorative impulse on my part.'

Color-coordinated *Wire* magazine covers. In the photo shoot for issue 17, Mouse on Mars were persuaded to wear matching green sweaters in anticipation of the CD sleeve (already in production) that would be attached to the cover.

The Wire Tapper CD sleeves: *16* was designed by Richard Rhys; *17* by Samuel Nyholm; and *18*, which was generated by replacing the cartridges in a color ink-jet printer with a row of felt-tip markers, was designed by Gerrit Rietveld Academie graduates Jaan Evart, Julian Hagen, and Daniël Maarleveld.

'I've always liked finding existing patterns in the environment and recognizing them as infinitely scalable and repeatable surfaces.'

Goggin often begins a project by zeroing in on a set of constraints and then working with or against them. This may explain his interest in patterns, with their engaging built-in systems. *Space Patterns* is a trio of patterns Goggin designed on commission for the UK art and photography magazine *Draft*. The patterns are thematically related through their titles, which are loosely connected to outer space. *Mars* is a translation of the pattern that is stamped on the bottom of Mars candy bars; *All-Star* was composed using the tread from Chuck Taylor sneakers; and *Univers* is a houndstooth typographic repeat of the letter *u* in Adrian Frutiger's Univers type in a variety of weights. Each pattern occupied a full page in the magazine.

As the art director of *Wire*, a British avant-garde music magazine, from 2005 to 2007, Goggin used color as a generative system for the design and photography that constantly shifted from issue to issue. In the two years he worked on the magazine he never repeated a cover color. Goggin enjoyed the challenge of art-directing the covers, which included commissioning sleeve designs for the CDs that were attached to the issues every six months.

One strong influence on Goggin's process has been his extensive collaborations with artists and curators, which have extended his perception of what graphic design can be. He understands the power of the visual cues in graphic design and uses them not to overpower, but rather to support larger ideas.

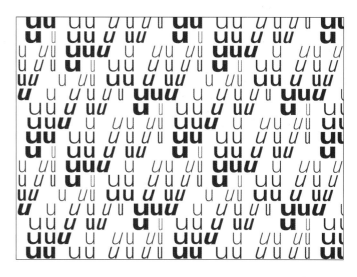

Space Patterns series designed for *Draft* magazine. From top to bottom: *Mars*, *All-Star*, and *Univers*.

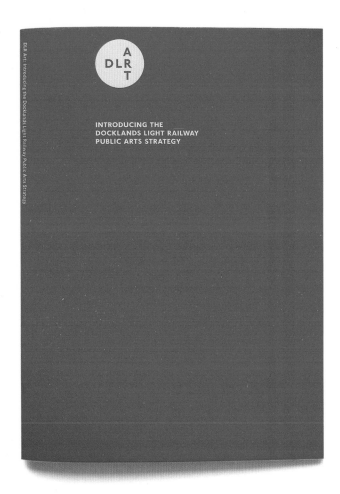

A
DLR
T

INTRODUCING THE
DOCKLANDS LIGHT RAILWAY
PUBLIC ARTS STRATEGY

In 2007, Goggin was commissioned to design an identity and signage system for London's Docklands Light Railway (DLR) Public Arts Programme. The DLR, part of London's public transportation system, is an elevated automated train system that runs from the City to the east and southeast. The Public Arts Programme was launched on the occasion of the DLR's twentieth anniversary, with the goal of extending the privilege of seeing art to everyone riding the train.

Goggin almost immediately chose red as the primary visual component of the system because it was the most explicit signifier of the railway. As the elevated train cars of the DLR pass through the landscape, along the Thames and against the sky, their red color is by far their most singular characteristic. Given the turquoise and blue scheme of the original DLR identity, red was the obvious missing color.

Extending his logic, Goggin drew upon the familiar framework of Transport for London's identity system, with its simple anatomy of circles and bars, thinking of it as a 'kind of Duchampian readymade' with which to bring public art and the railway together. Goggin admits that the intersection of 'DLR' and 'art' was one of those solutions that pops into your head as a first idea, but shouldn't necessarily be discounted because of that fact. 'If you give any graphic designer the abbreviation "DLR" and the word "art," probably the first thing they'll do is join them together so you have the *R* in "DLR" and "art" linked together….That's the first idea you should throw out as a graphic designer because it's too obvious, but I quite liked being that obvious and making such a simple logo that, in a way, anyone could have done it. A classic criticism of contemporary art is "my five year old could have done that," and I kind of liked the idea of the logo being held to that criticism.'

Rather than introduce a completely new symbol for the DLR's Public Arts Programme, Goggin explored variations on the familiar Transport for London identity.

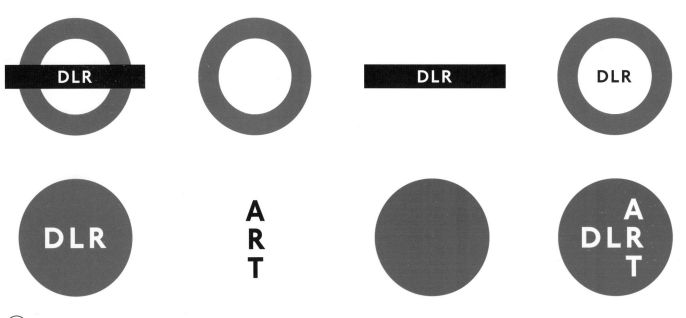

'The idea with this logo was an attempt to do nothing as a graphic designer. I would just take the given elements handed to me as part of the brief and then simply rearrange them—a kind of Duchampian ready-made approach where existing elements are recontextualized.'

The bright red carriages that distinguish the Docklands Light Railway are pictured in the DLR Public Arts Programme brochure.

Signage blends with existing station graphics. 'Something pointing out an artwork should feel just as commonplace as the arrow to the exit or the elevators,' Goggin says.

'I deliberately didn't want the logo to be too conceptual or decorative, because in my opinion that was the role of the art itself.'

Goggin further explained that his aim was to make a symbol that was as unobtrusive as possible. Rather than draw attention to itself, he wanted it to draw attention away from itself: 'I was looking at it the same way that I look at other graphic symbols like arrows or asterisks, which are almost anti-characters in the way that they direct attention away from themselves.' He simply wanted the logo to have just the necessary presence to signal that artwork was somewhere in the immediate vicinity.

For the labels and signage that would accompany the art installations, Goggin looked for 'the most mundane, expected materials possible,' appropriating the look of the existing poster casings in the stations and swapping out the word 'information' in official DLR green for the word 'art' in red. He also employed standard Transport for London baked-enamel signage for the new logo. For Goggin, incorporating the signage system into the existing vocabulary of station wayfinding took the DLR commission's goal of making art an everyday experience to its 'logical extreme.'

47% OF PEOPLE BELIEVE THE IDEA OF WEATHER IN OUR SOCIETY IS BASED ON CULTURE

53% BELIEVE IT IS BASED ON NATURE

The Unilever Series:
OLAFUR ELIASSON

16 October 2003 – 21 March 2004

Free Admission
Open Daily 10.00 – 18.00
Late nights Friday and Saturday until 22.00

Visit www.tate.org.uk
⊖ Southwark/Blackfriars

The Unilever Series:
an annual art commission sponsored by

Unilever

MODERN
TATE

Goggin's poster for Olafur
Eliasson's 2003 work *The
Weather Project* had the
customary restriction for
Tate Modern Turbine Hall
projects: the design must in
no way reveal the nature of
the installation prior to its
official opening.

Eliasson's ethereal installation
in the Turbine Hall was visited
by 2.3 million people during
the six months of the project.

'The design was actually an explicit diagram of what you were going see. In spite of the project's secrecy, I was essentially giving the game away already, something visitors wouldn't realize until they saw the installation.'

An economy of gesture is another fine-tuned aspect of Goggin's work, demonstrated in his graphics for Olafur Eliasson's 2003 installation *The Weather Project* at Tate Modern. The publicity for the annual Turbine Hall sculpture project is challenging because the Tate always keeps the installation a secret until opening day. Goggin was faced with the assignment to promote the soon-to-be-legendary installation, but with strict instructions not to give anything away.

He had only seen a mock-up of Eliasson's piece but understood that it was going to be an atmospheric minimalist installation, consisting of a yellow light and misty precipitation. He decided to graphically condense the concept into an equally minimalist design campaign using only type and color. The resulting design is astonishingly direct. Like the sun, the vast solid yellow of the picture plane charges your optic nerves and disorients them with particulate type that

feels like an afterimage of a headline that you were too blinded to fully see.

In Goggin's mind it was nothing more than 'a purely pragmatic selection of color.' He considered his reduced design to be almost a blueprint of the installation. The flooded yellow background simulated the massive yellow light of the gallery and the dotted rendition of the official Tate typeface acted as the mist.

To generate text for the announcement, he collaborated with Eliasson, who had commissioned the museum staff to fill out a pseudoscientific survey about their relationship with the weather. Statistics gleaned from the survey combined with some completely made-up facts provided arresting headlines for the campaign. A series of promotional postcards read, '8 out of 10 postcards mention the weather.' Goggin jokes, 'It seems quite likely that would be true, but we had no evidence of that.'

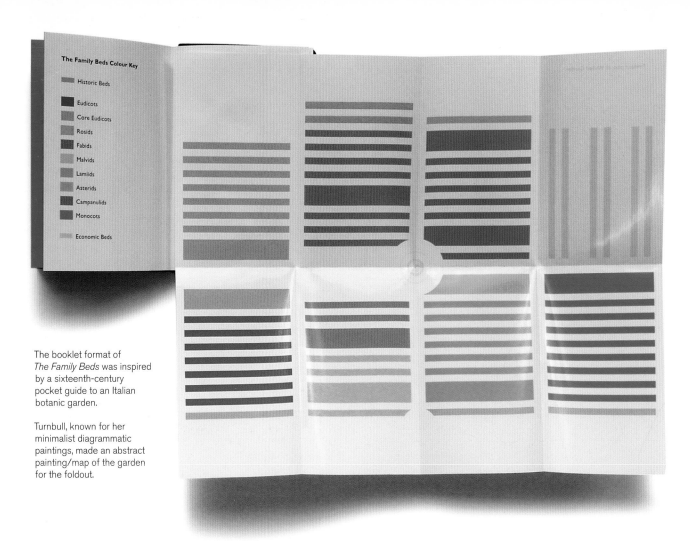

The Family Beds Colour Key

- Historic Beds
- Eudicots
- Core Eudicots
- Rosids
- Fabids
- Malvids
- Lamiids
- Asterids
- Campanulids
- Monocots
- Economic Beds

The booklet format of
The Family Beds was inspired
by a sixteenth-century
pocket guide to an Italian
botanic garden.

Turnbull, known for her
minimalist diagrammatic
paintings, made an abstract
painting/map of the garden
for the foldout.

'I can't claim pure objectivity. I'll
set up a system and then change
it at the last minute, breaking my
own rules.'

Goggin collaborated with artist Alison Turnbull on *The Family Beds*, which was conceived first as an artist's book but also functions as a practical guide to the University of Oxford Botanic Garden. The project grew from Turnbull's discovery, after visiting five European botanical gardens, of a scientific update in the way plants were classified. Turnbull found that Oxford University was planting the beds of its botanic garden according to the new genetic classifications rather than the customary arrangement of visual characteristics.

The format for the booklet was inspired by a pocket volume documenting a sixteenth-century Italian garden that Goggin and Turnbull discovered in the University of Oxford Library. Its pages contained a list of the plants in Latin with a corresponding engraved foldout map.

For Goggin and Turnbull, color-coding immediately came into play as the best way to visualize the structure of the

garden's new classification system—a different color for each plant family. The color palette for the project was ironically determined by the booklet's very basic paper stock: a cheap range of photocopy paper that Goggin had selected for its superior, bolder colors compared to more expensive designer papers.

Turnbull's drawings, paintings, and prints are often motivated by the geometry and symmetry of architectural plans, and this is reflected in the work she produced for the booklet: a plan of the Oxford garden that is both abstract painting and map. It was the office-paper color palette that ultimately informed Turnbull's arresting abstract painting. Scientists working on the new genetic botanical classification were so impressed with the color interpretation, they adopted it for use in their system. Goggin set Turnbull's work as a foldout map in the booklet in an echo of the sixteenth-century volume that had inspired them.

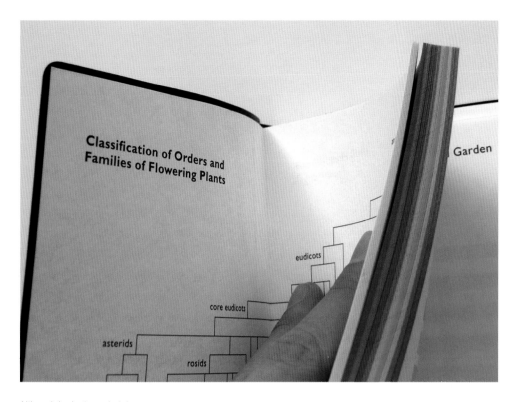

Although budget constraints dictated that the booklet be printed as basic black text on colored office copy paper, the rainbow-hued pages present a neatly color-coded guide to the University of Oxford Botanic Garden.

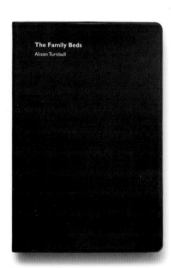

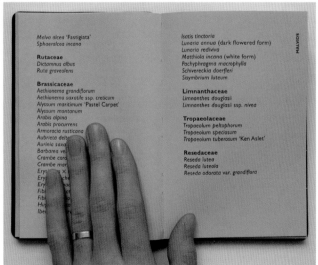

The PVC cover of the booklet was screen printed and bound by a company that makes diaries.

Not wanting to follow the model of the historic guide too literally, Goggin opted for a sans-serif typeface, choosing Gill Sans for its elegant italic font.

Creative DNA
James Goggin

As a student at London's Royal College of Art, James Goggin debated whether to be an artist or a designer. He attended lectures in architecture, fashion, and fine art, and was exposed to the Curating Contemporary Art program. His engagement with the contemporary art scene also helped to develop his ability to invent his own content for design projects.

In 1999, following his graduation, Goggin founded the graphic design studio Practise. His clients included Tate Modern, Camden Arts Centre, Barbican Art Gallery, Book Works, *Wire*, Phaidon, Transport for London, and David Kohn Architects.

After ten years in London, the Practise studio moved to Arnhem, the Netherlands, where Goggin combined commissioned projects with teaching at the Werkplaats Typografie in Arnhem and the Ecole cantonale d'art de Lausanne (ECAL), Switzerland.

Goggin has lectured and run workshops internationally at various institutions, including Split Fountain, Auckland; California Institute of the Arts, Los Angeles (CalArts); Walker Art Center, Minneapolis; ISIA Urbino; Iaspis, Stockholm; Gerrit Rietveld Academie, Amsterdam; and Hochschule Darmstadt. He regularly writes for international publications.

In August 2010, Goggin accepted the position of Director of Design, Print, and Digital Media at the Museum of Contemporary Art in Chicago, where he now lives and works.

drawing

3 Drawing

Drawing is the primary tool of the visual artist. It is a transformative action that links consciousness with the physical world, a feedback loop that merges hand, mind, and eye.

For both the directed individual and the more intuitive creator, drawing can help realize an intended solution or it can allow a concept to unfold like an unmapped journey, suggesting potential forms and meanings for further investigation. Drawing is a way of making connections between carefully constructed ideas and associations that may emerge as a designer works more spontaneously within the picture plane. It is a way to actualize both the unforeseen and the intentional; the ability to recognize what will be useful and shape or edit those discoveries is an equally critical part of the process.

Its efficiency in confronting communication problems early in a project is one of the primary reasons designers use drawing. Drawing facilitates the development of a focused visual grammar that depends on the complete understanding, by its creator, of all the elements required to construct an articulate visual language that will support all the messages intended to be communicated. Drawing is a valuable method for extracting that language from a larger field of thoughts and providing solid visual evidence of its possible success or failure within the project. Whether through a calculated and goal-driven approach or a more open-ended one, the distillation of ideas that are appropriate to the task at hand is what the designer intends to achieve through drawing.

The designers featured on the following pages are devoted to drawing as a working methodology. 'Thumbnails' shows how Michel Bouvet employs drawing to condense narratives into iconic pictures for theater posters, 'Sketchbooks' looks at the intuitive discovery process revealed in the perpetual sketchbooks of Ed Fella, and 'Type Design' explores how the contours of drawing help form Cyrus Highsmith's original typefaces.

Michel Bouvet

Thumbnails

Making thumbnail sketches is a time-tested method of visual problem solving. For poster designer Michel Bouvet, a thumbnail sketch simulates the directness of the poster, a medium that aims to distill an idea into an arresting visual expression for a mass public audience. Bouvet's clients are theatrical groups, and he works, through his drawings, to define a visual language from the text within each play that his posters will represent. These small sketches become miniposters, quick arrangements of signs, symbols, and typography forcing a stripped-down clarity that can reveal the effectiveness of one concept over another.

As someone with a serious interest in writing and theater, Bouvet has an exceptional affinity for the subjects he is portraying; before sitting down to sketch, he reads each playscript three or four times. If the play is contemporary and experimental, on the first read-through, Bouvet concedes, he may understand nothing; on the second read-through he will grasp the story, and on the third or fourth he will try to identify core concepts from the text, looking for the metaphors that will translate best into a visual language, allowing him to portray the story graphically without telling the end. His goal is to create work that has public appeal and also reflects a 'designer's spirit.' He recognizes that his charge with each poster is to 'communicate one of the world's best creations.' He strives to capture the sense and spirit of each play, as well as the directors' and choreographers' translation of the work onto the stage.

'I feel I'm in a world, not a flat piece of paper.'

Bouvet's final poster design must be strong enough to attract attention quickly in busy Paris streets and Métro stations.

eating a fish bone

leaking aquarium

standing in the sky

coffee erupting

hedgehog balancing

pot boiling over

tractor being tracked by radar

blowing bubbles from a horn

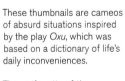

overflowing letter box

butter fracturing melba toast

fish tail in fire

fish escaping bowl

These thumbnails are cameos of absurd situations inspired by the play *Oxu*, which was based on a dictionary of life's daily inconveniences.

The uniformity of the thumbnails and their systematic arrangement on a presentation board allows for easy and evenhanded comparison.

mosquito buzzing in ear

chair farting

hedgehog with cactus

'You have to make concrete something which is very complicated. Thousands and thousands of words. You have to simplify.'

Once the direction for the drawing is approved, Bouvet makes dozens of variations before settling on the final.

The finished propped-up table leg thumbnail.

Bouvet's thumbnails are generated at home, away from the studio, often on a Sunday afternoon, with no phone calls, and only his cats for company. He doesn't aim for only one idea, but keeps working and concentrating until he has fourteen to twenty different ideas. He then discusses these ideas with his client, laying them out on a large table, and through a process of elimination the strongest three or four wil be identified for further development. The scope of the search evidenced in Bouvet's presentation sparks a conversation that helps to turn the client/designer relationship into a partnership, building trust and making the client comfortable with the direction the design will take.

Bouvet used this working method to design a poster for *Oxu*, an experimental production staged by La Pépinière theater in Paris. *Oxu* is a three-person play based on a humorous dictionary of life's daily inconveniences (the three actors were also the authors of the book). The thumbnails that Bouvet generated in his brainstorming for the poster are cameos of situations inspired by the play. After presenting a board of thumbnails to his client, the image of the table with a propped-up leg was selected as being most evocative of the performance. The image of a familiar object in a makeshift state related the most directly to the absurd atmosphere of the play.

'I try to get to the point where I
have about 14 to 20 different ideas.
14 is about right, not 12, not 13....13
is an unlucky number.'

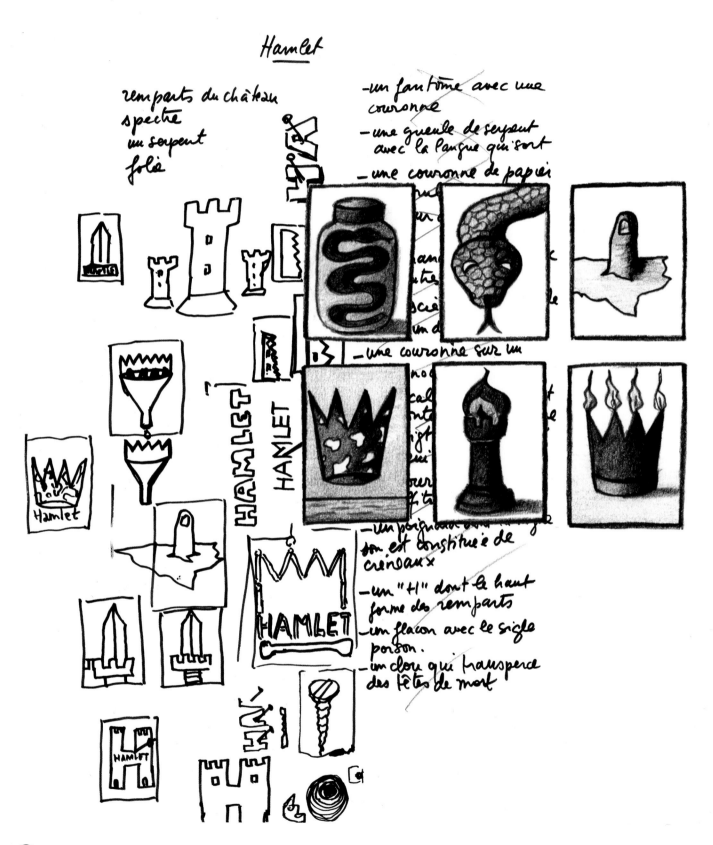

Bouvet partly attributes his interest in universal symbols to his extensive travels around the world where he has 'seen many posters that were simple enough to understand even without knowing the written language.' Finding a metaphor is often the best way to encapsulate meaning: for example, forming the letter *H* into a castle for Shakespeare's *Hamlet*. Bouvet's sketches show that the initial idea he investigated was the rook, a chess piece also called the castle or tower, suggesting to Bouvet both the setting of *Hamlet* and the strategies and machinations in evidence throughout the play. By translating this iconic chess piece into a monumental *H*, Bouvet is able to create a simultaneous reading of image and text that embodies the potency of the play.

Bouvet knows his final designs must be strong enough to immediately capture peoples' interest in busy Paris streets and Métro stations. At the same time, he likes to provide a second and third level of detail, a more elaborate reading for the viewer to discover as they move closer. In Bouvet's words: 'I really like it when a poster is just like pow, boom, and you never get tired of it…you can look at it and discover new things over time.' The idea that every poster contains a primary and secondary concept is an essential part of each design he creates. Bouvet maintains that because every piece of great literature possesses a great depth of symbolism, it is critical to connote these qualities through the selection of appropriate images. To him that is the most important role for the designer.

Initial sketches for Bouvet's *Hamlet* poster for Théâtre Les Gémeaux tested a range of powerful metaphorical images to express the essence of the play.

'What is the most important part of the story? Not telling the end.'

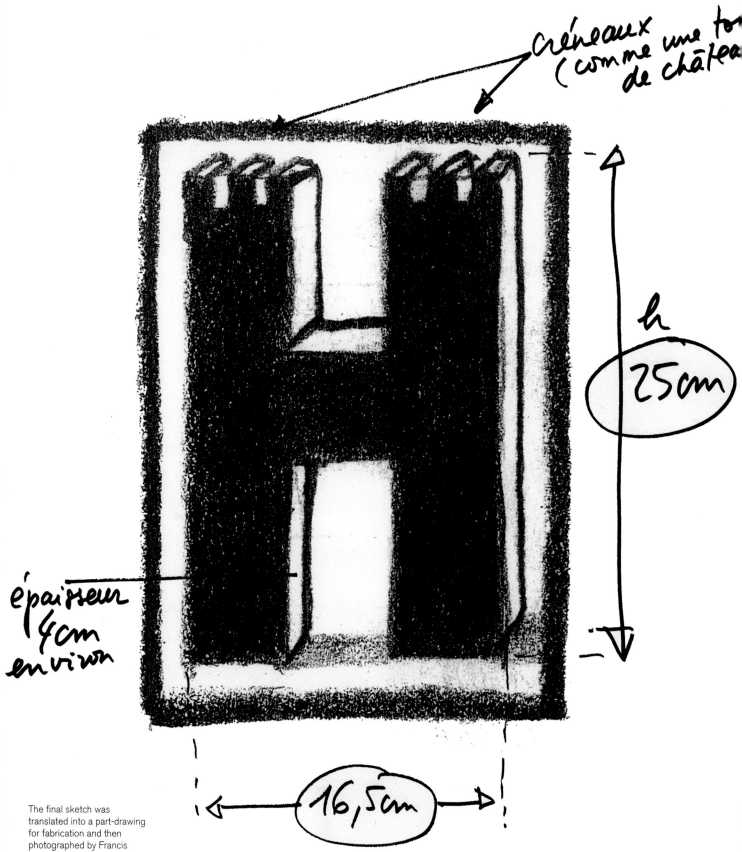

créneaux (comme une to(r)
(comme une to(r)
de châtea(u)

h
25cm

épaisseur
4cm
environ

16,5cm

The final sketch was
translated into a part-drawing
for fabrication and then
photographed by Francis
Laharrague in stark black
and white to fit the signature
poster style for Théâtre
Les Gémeaux.

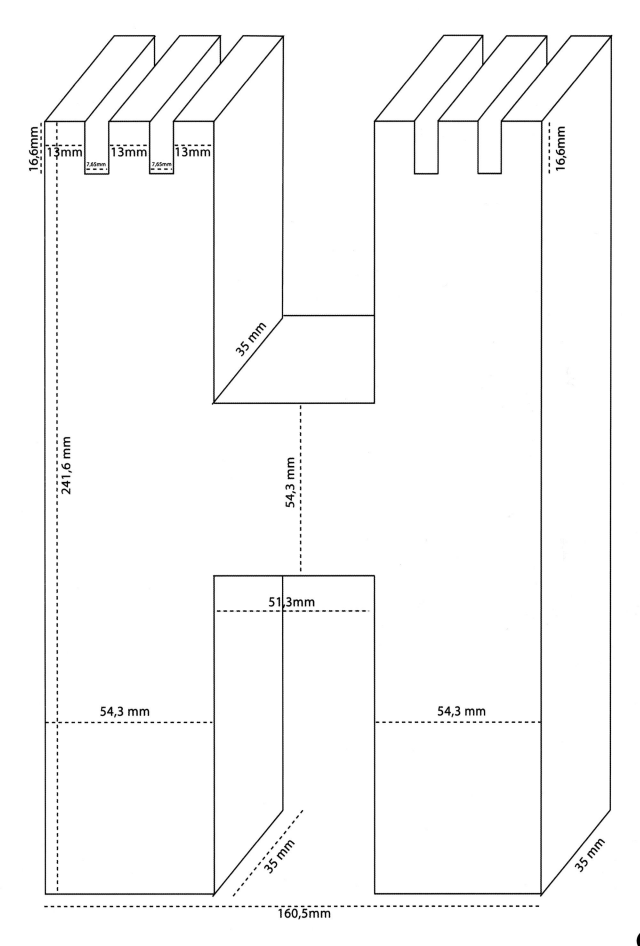

As Bouvet finalizes the details of the poster he works to harmonize all of the elements, especially the typography. 'Typography has a kind of sound. I feel that within the title of each play every word has a special sound both when you say it and when you see the word. Every title has to be transformed into something that is absolutely close to the spirit of the word.' As he works out the typography he builds on the strength and meaning he has assembled in the image. For the *Hamlet* poster, Bouvet redrew the serifs of the Clarendon title to mimic the imposing architecture of the castle. Within the homogeneity of the overall feel of the piece he provides a second read of the title in a shadowy script, suggesting duplicity and further complexity.

Looking at the detail in the final *Hamlet* poster, beautifully executed as a black-and-white photograph by Francis Laharrague to fit the distinctive poster style Bouvet established for Théâtre Les Gémeaux, it is hard to believe that it started out as a thumbnail. The unintimidating scale of this device makes it a natural starting point for designers. A few inches of paper provide a laboratory for experimentation. Bouvet has extended this small, safe space to his clients, inviting them in to participate.

The three-dimensional scale model cast in plaster and photographed by Francis Laharrague.

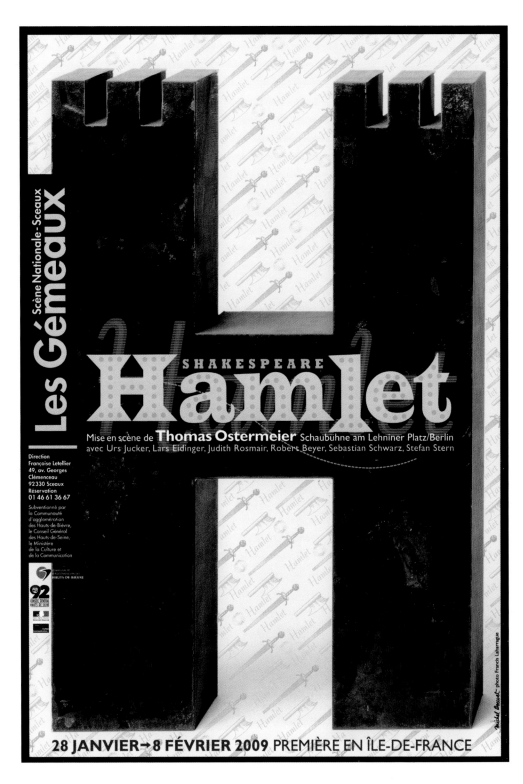

Bouvet's final poster for the Théâtre Les Gémeaux production of *Hamlet* condenses several symbols into one.

Creative DNA
Michel Bouvet

Michel Bouvet was exposed to the life and activities of artists at a very young age through summer visits to the Berry studio of his aunt and uncle, both renowned ceramicists. While visiting them, he was also introduced to a painter/illustrator who fascinated Bouvet with his paper cuts.

Bouvet received a diploma in painting from the Ecole nationale supérieure des Beaux-Arts in Paris. As an art student he was inspired by the work of painters Matisse, Pollock, Léger, and Savignac, as well as by contemporary French and American photographers. These influences came together perfectly in the form of the poster, which Bouvet sees as not only a sheet of paper but a canvas.

While photographing in the snow on a trip to Prague in 1977, Bouvet found his attention directed to colorful theater posters in the streets. This was a turning point in his career; even though his photographs were well received, he decided to concentrate on the poster as a means of expression.

Bouvet finds inspiration in books, newspapers, music, cinema, photography, and discussions with his wife, Anita, who is a painter. He teaches at the Ecole supérieure de design, d'art graphique et d'architecture intérieure (ESAG) Penninghen, Paris.

His poster designs have won major awards, including the Grand Prize for a Cultural Poster, Bibliothèque Nationale, Paris; first prize at the International Poster Biennale, Fort Collins, Colorado; a silver medal at the International Poster Triennal, Toyama, Japan; and the Jan Lenica Prize, International Poster Biennale, Warsaw.

Ed Fella

Sketchbooks

Creativity demands the ability to move back and forth between expansive thinking and close editing. Sketchbooks are an essential means by which designers catalog their thoughts. Without these notebooks, spontaneous observations that are often the origins of innovative thinking may be forgotten. Ed Fella believes there are many different kinds of creativity and creative processes, and that each type of design problem calls for its own course of action. His mantra for his sketchbooks has always been 'Execution before conception. Meaning before perception'—a slogan he developed many years ago when he began keeping these books, which were based on the objective of 'doing something without knowing what you are doing.'

'Execution before conception.
Meaning before perception.'

This recent sketchbook was drawn with a four-cartridge plastic ball-point pen and contains eighteen drawings of each color, beginning with blue, then red, black, and green.

Fella's personal sketchbooks are a deconstruction of the commercial art forms and techniques that he mastered while working in Detroit on advertising and promotion for the automobile industry, banks, and pharmaceutical companies. They only exist 'after the fact' of the commercial artwork that he did seriously day and night for thirty years. While there are probably thousands of pages in the sketchbooks, Fella speculates that there are probably thousands more if you count all of the ideas he generated while he was working, 90% of which were never used. 'I worked to order like a machine for thirty years...now I'm still making widgets but there are no more blueprints.'

Fella picks a letter or a word out of the air and builds from there, often combining words into compact sayings. Like automatic writing, there is a sequence, something in mind 'that just kind of goes along' as he letters it. In this process of 'execution before conception,' he has intentionally turned the design process upside down. Instead of beginning with a problem, getting an idea, and then developing it, an image doesn't emerge until the instant he begins to sketch it, and his perception of how its meaning is unfolding doubles back to motivate the next move on the page.

'Rackets red Clearly' was a word play on the lyric 'rockets' red glare,' from 'The Star-Spangled Banner.'

   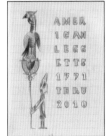  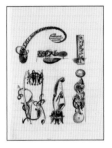

Sometimes there is no meaning behind Fella's sketches, just bits and pieces of letterform shapes—subconscious artifacts from his advertising career.

In making this sketch, Fella drew the letters *C*, *A*, and *T*; not fond of cats, Fella escaped that word by moving on to 'catalog,' reinforcing it with a rebus of 'log,' which directed his stream of consciousness to 'fir.'

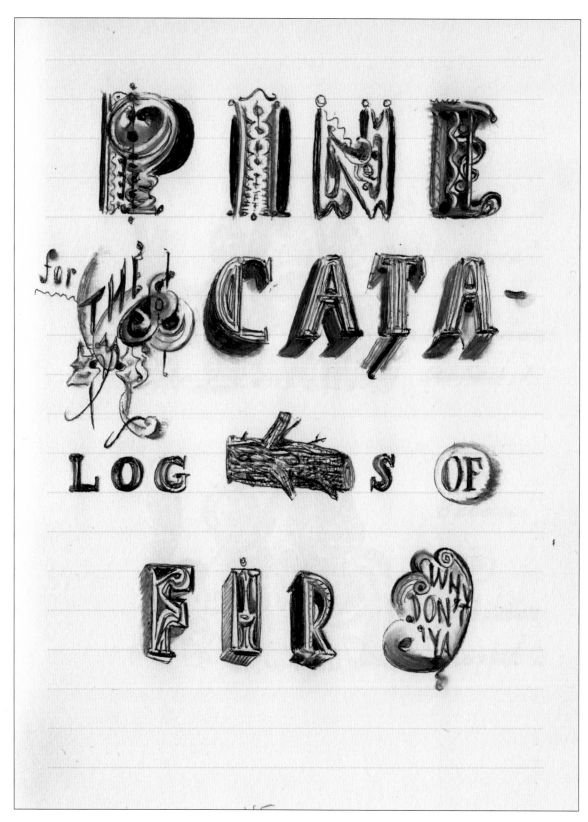

There is no such thing as a mistake to Fella. Obliterated fragments evolve into new forms on the page.

Fella uses a white Prismacolor pencil on top of the ball-point pen ink before it dries to add dimension and softness to his images.

The final drawings in this sketchbook combine all the inks in the four-color pen. This is usually the case in Fella's other sketchbooks, but this one is an exception: the colors are separated until the last few pages.

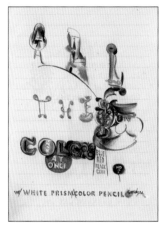

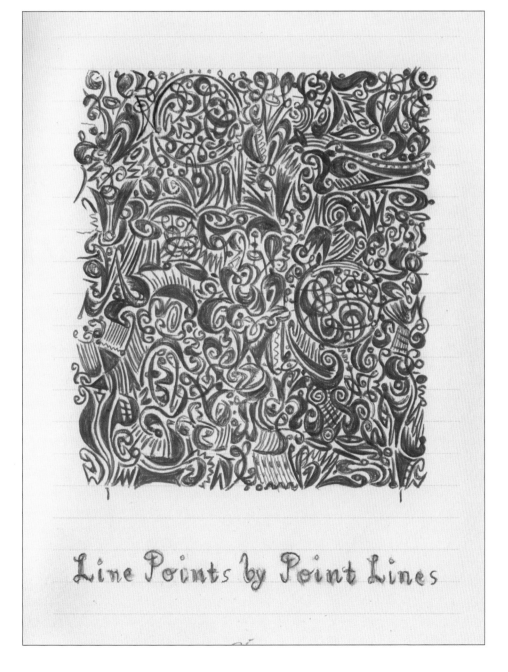

Is this what will never do because do is what this never will.

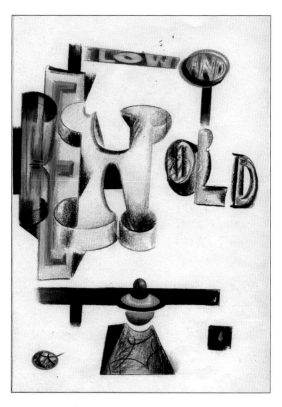

Low and behold.

10,000,000 years from now—then.

Mind your P's and Q's & A's. Ta ta it's O.K.

This personal sketchbook took Fella ten years of off-and-on work between 1989 and 1999. It is primarily typographic, based on deconstructed 'commercial art' lettering. The drawings were made with Prismacolor pencils and tools such as French curves and circle templates.

Words and pictures fuse into
pithy sayings. Many are easy to
decipher; others, like the one
above, are not meant to be.

Fella's drawings and graphic design work reflect his passion for vernacular hand-drawn lettering and illustration, and their built-in irregularities. His personal sketchbooks have always existed alongside his commercial work and there has been a constant to-and-fro between the two. He often extends the process from his experimental drawing into assignments for guest-lecture posters, his own speaking engagements, and other pro bono projects at the California Institute of the Arts (CalArts).

Fella's 'stream of consciousness' methodology was at work in a T-shirt design for the 2010 Student Conference of the American Institute of Graphic Arts (AIGA) at CalArts. After playing with various combinations of type and shape, working with the saying 'What goes around comes around,' he provoked a further meaning as he set the type on top of a square, prompting him to modify the saying to 'What goes around doesn't come back round.'

'I hand lettered an alphabet and, after photocopying as many copies as I needed, I cut out and pasted down the individual letters to spell out the text. The original triangle, circle, square breakdown is now a cliché for design teaching first used by the Bauhaus. After it was all put together I noticed that "around" was in a square, so I dropped the *a*, which gave the idea a clever visual twist.'

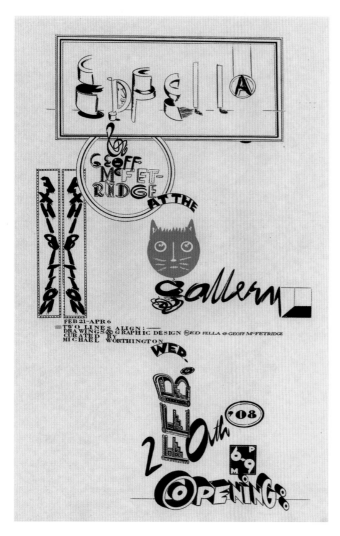

Announcement, front and back, for the opening of an Ed Fella and Geoff McFetridge exhibition at REDCAT, Los Angeles, 2008.

abcdefghijklm:
nopqrstuxwvyz

doesn't
come back
around

Fella's design for the 2010
CalArts T-shirt auction. Each
year students and faculty design
sixty to seventy shirts, which are
auctioned to raise money for the
AIGA student chapter.

Creative DNA
Ed Fella

Even though his work is highly intuitive, Ed Fella questions the premise of 'intuition.' He believes that so-called spontaneity has to come from something—in his case, years of studying, making, and teaching art and design.

In his early childhood, Fella took art classes at the Detroit Institute of Arts, which were sometimes held in Diego Rivera Court, where he and the other young students would be surrounded by Rivera's awe-inspiring murals.

At fifteen, Fella's began at Detroit's Cass Technical High School. The school's commercial art program was based on the Bauhaus and made no distinction between functional and fine art. The program also had a rigorous art history curriculum. As he studied each period from the Renaissance to the twentieth century, Fella noticed that each consecutive movement—Cubism, Surrealism, Dadaism, etc.—seemed perpetually in opposition to the one before. Ever since, Fella has seen creativity as 'always trying to be the opposite.' At eighteen, Fella began his commercial career at one of Detroit's biggest art studios, while taking evening adult-education courses in art appreciation, poetry, and literature at Wayne State University.

Fella met Katherine McCoy in the late 1960s at Designers and Partners in Detroit; later, when she moved on with her husband, Michael McCoy, to head the design program at the nearby Cranbrook Academy of Art, Fella was a favorite visiting critic. Fella officially attended Cranbrook's graduate program from 1985 to 1987, and upon receiving his MFA, accepted a position at CalArts, where he presently teaches.

Cyrus Highsmith

Type Design

When Cyrus Highsmith sees a page set in one of his typefaces, he sees thousands of his drawings arranged on a two-dimensional surface. His preoccupation with drawing began when he was young, with his mother, an artist, teaching him about negative space. She taught him 'that if you draw the space between the branches of the tree, you end up with a tree that looks a lot more like a tree than if you try to just draw the branches.'

While Highsmith is capable of crafting revivals of historical typefaces, he is most passionate about generating original forms. Unlike revivals, which come with their own stories and rendering techniques—such as the stroke and stress of a pen point—new typefaces require a lot of imagination to establish their purpose and determine the best way to formally reflect it.

Highsmith locates his graphic approach somewhere between contour drawing and letterpress printing: 'What I'm really interested in is shape, contour, and white space. The way I draw is kind of ahistorical and not very calligraphic. Generally I draw white space first and put at least equal impor- tance, if not more, on that.' In activating the white space, he considers it at every location: 'Imagine a paragraph of text. There is counterspace—the space inside the letter; letter space—the space between letters; and line

'Calligraphy is nice because it's not mechanical, but what interests me about type is that it is mechanical.'

Highsmith's typeface Daley's Gothic, named after his mother, has compact spaces that amplify and activate the white space.

Highsmith explores positive and negative space in this abstract form 'drawn' with scissors and paper and pasted into one of his sketchbooks.

space—the space between the lines; and you can attach all those things to the letter....I call that space the "glyph space."' He describes the spaces between letters in relation to foundry type, where the letters are situated on fixed modular areas of open space: 'I really like movable type for that reason as opposed to calligraphy. I like the mechanical nature of it and how the modularity simplifies that space and how it lets things repeat in an interesting way. That's what makes type not calligraphy.'

When Highsmith is designing on commission, he establishes the personality and audience of the publication, and specific requirements for the type's use in the layouts—its size, color, and surrounding typefaces. These constraints are critical in helping him define a project's direction.

The challenge in designing original typefaces is to invent the requirements. He will simply begin by imagining a publication or use for his type. 'I think about it as a way of storytelling. A typeface plays a role always in a story, so in a way I think of the story it's going to be a part of. I don't mean it has to illustrate something from the story—it could represent the voice of the author, the publisher; it could evoke the setting; it could be something to do with one of the characters; there are a lot of ways to do it. There's also the functionality—the usage—which is important, but to me the interesting part is what story the typeface is part of and what's its role in that story?' He notes that this method is similar to the process that designers go through when they choose a typeface.

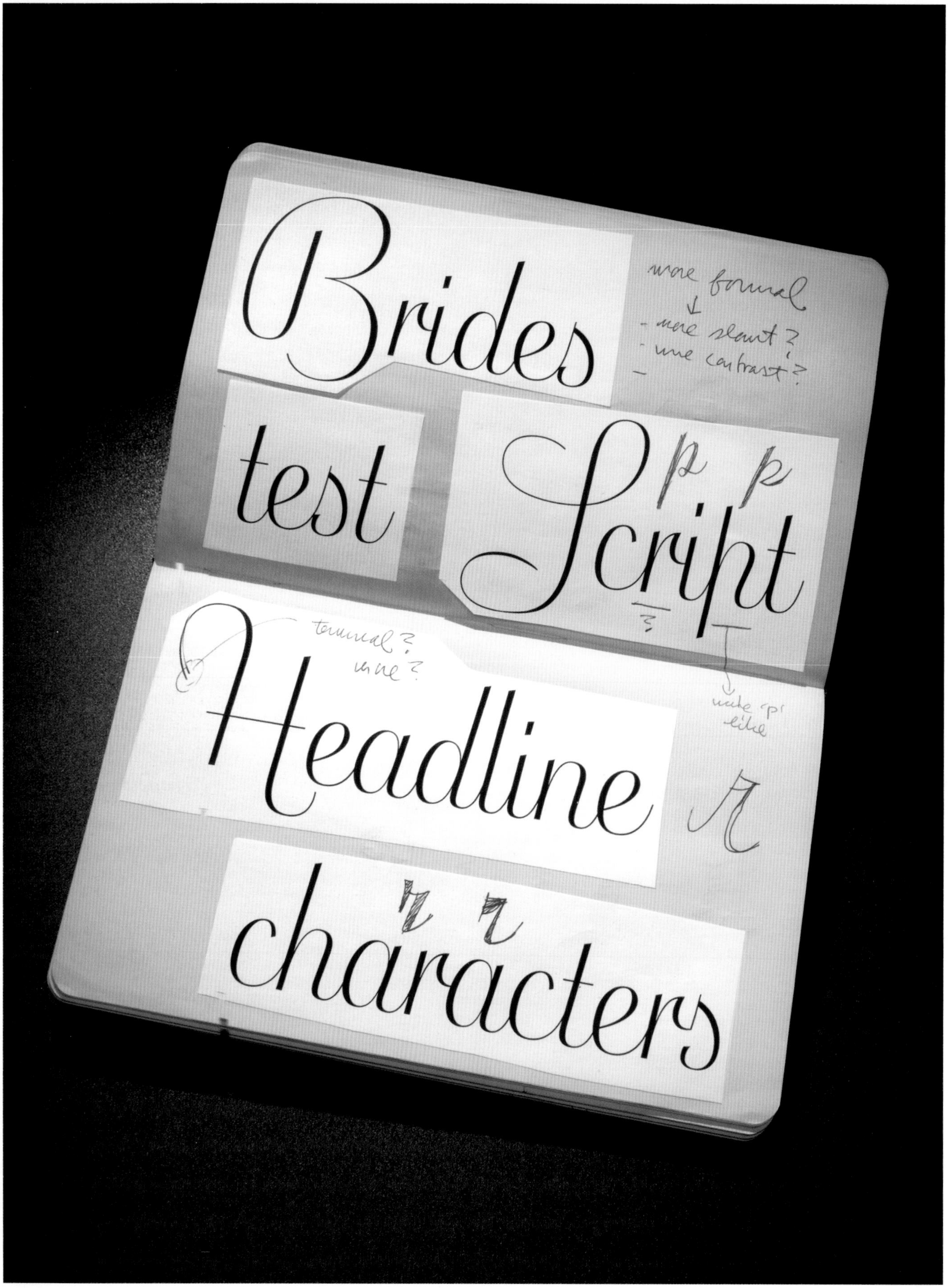
Brides
test
Script
Headline
characters

Highsmith's sketchbook matrix of possible styles for Biscotti, showing three basic scripts: informal, formal, and constructed.

Facing page: Notations on a test proof of Biscotti show modifications for characters *p* and *r*.

'I think with my drawing you see a lot of repetition, but that's how I figure stuff out.'

One example of a typeface designed on commission is the script Biscotti. Originally developed for *Brides* magazine, this project was initially a little outside of Highsmith's comfort zone, too calligraphic and feminine for his style. The art director quickly, and brilliantly, helped Highsmith get his head around it with a simple directive: 'I want a typeface that makes me feel pretty.'

'When I sketch,' says Highsmith, 'this is about as final as I will get. I don't do careful drawings by hand and then careful drawings in the computer, because to me that's twice as much work.'

Highsmith works with art directors who know type at a high level and can evaluate options with an advanced typographic vocabulary. In order to locate the script's personality, he constructed a simple matrix in his sketchbook to discuss at the meeting. He developed three basic styles: an informal brush script that might be found on a sign; a formal engraved or pen script, reminiscent of a wedding invitation; and a more constructed, mechanical script, like chrome lettering on a car. The three styles were displayed in three columns, progressively more slanted. Highsmith identified a correlation between the amount of slant and the perceived degree of formality and concluded that the more slanted the letters were, the more formal they appeared.

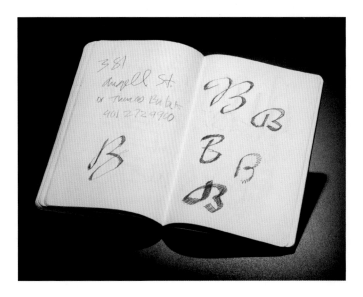

He narrowed his focus to the wedding-invitation style and looked for a slant that wasn't 'too grandmotherly' and would appeal to 'young brides who want to make their grandmothers happy, but still want it to be their own thing,' ending up with the modest slant from the middle column of the matrix.

Highsmith begins a design by drawing in his sketchbooks until he has a general idea, but he quickly moves to working on the computer, seeing careful work in the sketchbook followed by careful drawings on the computer as a needless duplication of effort. He translates the forms in his sketchbooks to the computer by eye rather than by scanning them in and tracing.

As a rule, he avoids looking at other typefaces as much as possible during his design process, unless he is working out something specific and needs to see how other people solved a detail of a problem. In the case of the cursive Biscotti, he looked at some similar typefaces to see how some of the connections between letters were resolved. Highsmith encourages his students to work the same way, not looking at other typefaces while designing.

Highsmith's concentration on white space is evident in the counterforms of Biscotti. He sees a different shade of white outside the letter than inside. To explain this, he sketches around the letter *T* to illustrate how the intensity of white varies in the shapes surrounding the letter. As he draws the curves he looks at the counterforms without thinking about the weight of the line between the forms. 'It's a line in some ways, but it's really not a line, it's a very thin contour. I think about the two sides as two different things.'

'When you're drawing a line you're defining an edge, and an edge is the border between two shapes, so you are drawing them both at once, which is not unique to type by any means.'

Alternative forms are explored as printouts are made at each phase of the project.

REGULAR

BOLD

REGULAR

White space is an important part of the composition of every letter. Highsmith sketches around the counterform of the letter *T* to illustrate how the intensity of white varies in the shapes surrounding the letter.

BISCOTTI AVAILABLE FROM FONT BUREAU AND ITS DISTRIBUTORS

REGULAR — *Wedlock*

BOLD — *Heavy Congestion on Lovers' Lane*

REGULAR — *Vows Blooper Reel*

BOLD — *Tuxedo*

REGULAR — *Klezmer Music*

BOLD — *Pronounced man & wife by accordian player*

Biscotti was commissioned in 2004 by Gretchen Smelter and Donna Agajanian for *Brides* magazine. "We want a typeface that makes the reader feel pretty; it should capture the voice of this happy occasion." Cyrus Highsmith has prepared a radically simple descendant of the flourished engraved scripts traditionally deemed suitable for such formal occasions, a 21st century typeface that captures the smiling spirit of these classical forms; FB 2007

2 STYLES: REGULAR AND BOLD

CRYSTAL GAZING

COMPRESSED BLACK

Live in the future, forget about the past

CONDENSED REGULAR ITALIC

MYSTERIOUS FORCES

BOLD

Palm readers

WIDE LIGHT

BLACK CATS KEEP CROSSING MY PATH

CONDENSED BLACK ITALIC

FUTURE

COMPRESSED BLACK

I am plagued by an ancient curse

LIGHT

WALKING THE EARTH

COMPRESSED MEDIUM ITALIC

No place to stop and rest

WIDE REGULAR

DOOMED FOR ETERNITY

CONDENSED BLACK

Old soothsayers warned me to be careful

REGULAR ITALIC

Relay reaches back to the middle of the last century for inspiration. In England, Edward Johnston and Eric Gill applied humanist structures to the geometric sans, establishing a trend within European art deco. In the US, W.A. Dwiggins achieved a similar effect with Metro, influencing lettering from the diner to the comic book. Cyrus Highsmith, a lifelong fan of the comics, has designed a spirited new series in this tradition. FB 2002

40 STYLES: LIGHT, REGULAR, MEDIUM, BOLD AND BLACK WEIGHTS
IN COMPRESSED, CONDENSED, NORMAL AND WIDE WIDTHS, ALL WITH ITALICS

A complementary example to client-commissioned Biscotti is Relay, a type family with a 1940s feel, in various weights, designed on Highsmith's own creative initiative. The motivation for this typeface was twofold. First, he had always loved geometric sans serifs, but saw areas for improvement. Futura, one of his favorites, lost its personality when it was too heavily bolded or used in a condensed width. He liked Kabel, but wanted to design something less specifically Art Deco–looking. He also looked at Metro and Erbar, which were less geometric, as influences. Highsmith felt the need for a big family of sans serifs, inspired by the anonymous typefaces of the machine age, 'something you might see on a newspaper in a thirties or forties movie, but slicker.'

The second part of the inspiration for the typeface was his wife Anna. 'I wanted to draw a typeface for Anna, my wife, that she could use and that was her style, so she was the character behind the design.' He specifically sees her personality in the regular and wide versions of

Relay: 'To my eye it's kind of feminine, but not too girly. I wanted it to be kind of pretty.' The success of Highsmith's contemporary but feminine geometric font is validated by its use in many women's magazines.

Highsmith works on several projects at a time, so it is hard for him to estimate how long it took to design all forty variations of Relay, which include light, regular, medium, bold, and black weights in compressed, condensed, normal, and wide widths, all with corresponding italics, but he guesses it was six months' to a year's worth of work. When asked if there is a customary weight that is the starting point of his typefaces, he says there is no definite way to begin, but that it depends on the design: 'Sometimes you start in the middle and work your way out, and sometimes you start at the ends, and work your way in.' Once the initial weights are designed, there are interpolating algorithms that can be used to generate bolder or lighter weights, compressed or wider widths, etc., but some will still need to be drawn, and all will be refined.

Facing page: Highsmith's Relay was inspired both by shortcomings he perceived in other sans-serif typefaces and by his wife, Anna, whom he sees as 'the character behind the design.'

R

Futura
Paul Renner
1927

R

Metro
William Addison Dwiggins
1936

R

Kabel
Rudolph Koch
1927

R

Erbar
Jakob Erbar
1926

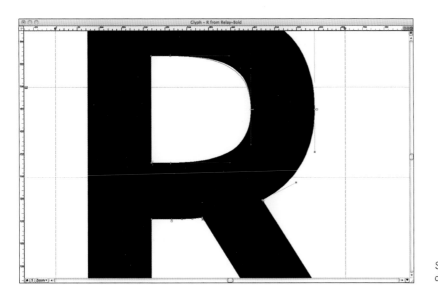

'It's rare that you get an art director who says, "Oh, I need a new typeface" when they're doing a redesign....They have probably tried a lot of existing typefaces and maybe they work, maybe they don't work, maybe they like some things about the way it works and not others, and eventually they'll get to a spot where they'll call me.'

Screen shot of Relay being drawn with FontLab software.

'I like drawing fonts but I also do a lot of other drawing. I do cartoons. Most people are familiar with my typefaces, and when they see my drawings they say they look like letters. To me my letters look like my drawings.'

Highsmith keeps lists of words that he likes and sometimes uses these to name his creations; his wife, Anna, also helps him. Sometimes the name of a typeface comes to him while he's drawing it. For Relay, he was thinking of the many different definitions of the word: communication, a switch, electronics. (By coincidence, capital *R* is also one of his favorite letters.)

Highsmith's drawing is not limited to typeface design: his sketchbooks betray his avid love for comics and cartoons. He says, 'In cartooning there are a lot of really simple drawings, they all fit together, they all look like they are part of the same world, and that world can extend beyond the page. You can imagine what a car might look like in a cartoon, even if there's not a drawing of one. I think that's true of any good typeface: you can imagine what the other letters look like even if you don't see them.'

An octopus rendered in Highsmith's sketchbook with stencil and rubber stamping. The gesture of rubber stamping—its repetition, speed, and lack of direct control—is like drawing, and its modularity is similar to typography.

Pages from Highsmith's
sketchbooks, 'where I do
my thinking.'

Creative DNA
Cyrus Highsmith

Excited by the proliferation of original typefaces in the early 1990s, Cyrus Highsmith, then a student at the Rhode Island School of Design (RISD), took as many independent studies as he could to pursue typeface design. Highsmith graduated with honors from RISD in 1997 and joined the Font Bureau. Now a senior designer, he concentrates on the development of new type series.

Highsmith also teaches typography in the Graphic Design department at RISD. He lectures and gives workshops across the United States, Mexico, and Europe. In 2001, Highsmith was featured in *Print* magazine's New Visual Artist Review. His typefaces Prensa and Relay were among the winners at Bukva:Raz!, the international type design competition.

His fonts include Amira, Antenna, Benton Sans, Biscotti, Caslon's Egyptian, Daley's Gothic, Dispatch, Eggwhite, Escrow, Heroun Sans, Ibis Display, Ibis Text, Loupot, Miller Headline, Novia, Occupant Gothic, Prensa, Quiosco, Receiver, Relay, Salvo Sans, Salvo Serif, Scout, Stainless, and Zocalo.

He is currently collaborating with writer Miguel Antón and designer Joancarles Casasín from Spain on a graphic novel, *Nothing of Consequence*.

narrative

4 Narrative

Narrative as a communication tool is central to the graphic design process. First, it locates us within the context of history, culture, and personal events and builds a knowledge base for us to mine as we further contribute to its evolution. Second, it is a universal model that we can manipulate to form effective vehicles of communication. Finally, it offers a framework within which we are the protagonist of our own design endeavors.

Narrative helps to focus the design process. The story, with its conventional arcing structure from beginning to middle to end, is a holistic and universal form that is understood by all. The designer can employ this structural framework to craft a path for the reader/viewer. Editing and sequencing, both critical parts of the design process, help to shape this path. Storytelling can provide the foundation for short or long, simple or complex messages and can be expressed through any medium—still or time-based, linear or nonlinear. Even a discrete moment can be taken from a narrative and translated into a powerful image.

Stories can also be used to generate ideas during the design process. For example, students in a design class were asked to arrange colored sticks on a square piece of white board to illustrate principles of composition such as asymmetry, balance, and rhythm. In less than a minute one student crafted an elegant composition for 'asymmetry' by fanning out sticks around the edge of the square. When asked how she completed such a beautiful piece in such a short time, the student modestly explained that she had told herself a quick story that the sticks were being repelled by a magnet underneath the table.

'Narrative' features two design studios that use stories as a means of discovery. Lorraine Wild, founder of Green Dragon Office, uses the form of the book to re-present the work and motivations of contemporary artists whose processes are themselves often informed by the code systems of narrative. Me Company pushes the potential of computer-generated forms to stage vivid imaginary stories that enliven the world of fashion design.

4.1

Lorraine Wild

Book Design

The form of the book—its material qualities, its tactile presence, the inherent effort in its making and distribution—evokes reverence, especially among graphic designers. It is bound and so finite, tactile, and so tangible; it represents labor, a serious undertaking, and ultimately a realization. But how does an exquisite book take shape?

'Everyone's life, like everyone's creative process, is a narrative.'

For Lorraine Wild, founder of Green Dragon Office, books are a vehicle for preserving visual memory and her aim is to use every element of a book, however insignificant it might seem, to make its content manifest in its physical appearance. Her recent projects are almost exclusively art books and monographs created for prestigious museums in Los Angeles, where many working artists are already becoming important historic figures.

She approaches each project as a collaboration between the artist, the institution, and herself. Most of her books accompany curated shows and contain a balance of essays, criticism, and plates of the artworks. Her experience teaching graphic design has helped her in the process of translating these varied viewpoints and media into a visual narrative. The process of extracting the essence of the work, its scale, and its color into book form is, to use her word, 'diagnostic.' She looks closely and listens intently to understand what the core of interest is in the work. After carefully analyzing its qualities she asks, 'How can the book stabilize that, archive that?' She also acknowledges that 'many ideas that artists have don't translate very well into book form,' so she does her best to get at the issues behind the work and then consider how they can be conceptualized and ultimately visualized.

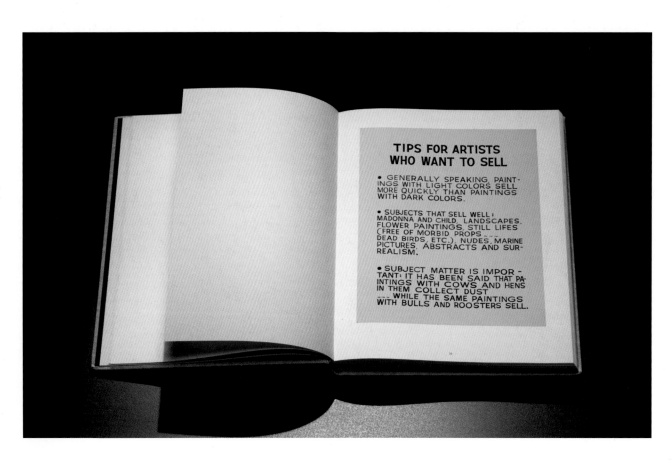

This simple cover design for a John Baldessari exhibition catalog was an homage to the handwritten type found in Baldessari's paintings.

Wild's books have a powerful physical presence and reflect tremendous attention to detail, from size, weight, and proportion to color and texture.

Generally her first formal design action is to determine the proportions of the book. This process involves many paper prototypes to test different sizes and shapes. Wild stresses that printouts are very important at every stage of the project because the screen is completely unreliable when it comes to translating any sense of scale, especially the nuances of typographic relationships. She asserts, 'Proportion is a physical thing, so it has to be a physical decision and not based on the screen.'

As part of her initial process Wild researches books that have already been published on a given subject, carefully evaluating their content and design. She was called upon in 2010 by the Los Angeles County Museum of Art to design the exhibition catalog for the retrospective *John Baldessari: Pure Beauty*. The first thing that came to mind was a show of Baldessari's monumental collages she had seen at the Margo Leavin Gallery. The work had incredible scale and the exhibition was a strong spatial experience that 'burnt a hole in her brain.'

In looking at earlier books on Baldessari, it was clear to Wild that the visual impact of his work was difficult to convey in book form, where compact pages are filled with text and images. In response to this challenge, she proposed a book layout in which the artwork would appear at the beginning in an isolated plate section without captions. In Wild's mind, 'this allowed the work to be appreciated completely on its own—essential and unembellished.'

'Much of the graphic design process behind the scenes of book design is invisible.'

'It's not his book and it's not my book....It shows several people thinking about his work and putting it into perspective.'

The half title page of the catalog was set on a narrow cut sheet of uncoated text stock before the introductory plate section.

Various 'voices' in the book were distinguished typographically as well as with paper and color.

The text was interleaved between color signatures on narrower uncoated pages.

The images in the plate section were meticulously sequenced, ending with film stills that segued perfectly into an essay on Baldessari's film work.

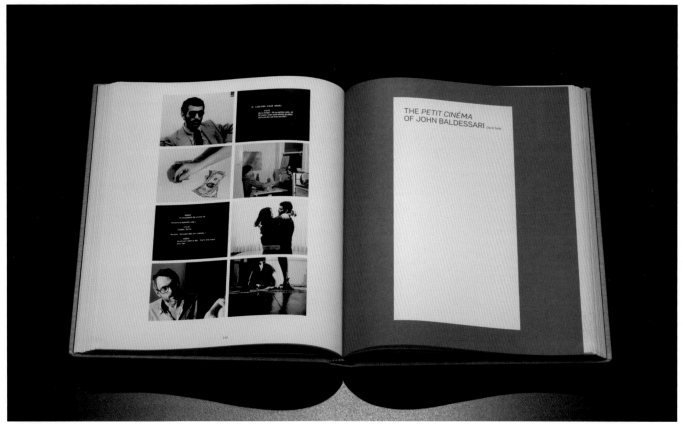

The essays were set in a one-column format in the typeface Galaxy by Village Typographers.

This double-page spread suggests a sequence of images on a gallery wall.

Another recent and favorite project of Wild's is a book on German artist Martin Kippenberger that accompanied his first major US retrospective exhibition, *Martin Kippenberger: The Problem Perspective*, at the Museum of Contemporary Art (MOCA), Los Angeles. Kippenberger's work spanned almost every medium—installations, photographs, posters, paintings, sculpture, and self-published books—and was multifarious in its content as well as in its approach.

Wild was instinctively drawn to MOCA curator Ann Goldstein's collection of books that Kippenberger had made to document his work. They were very basic documents, printed on standard office paper at a utility-level print shop in Germany. This was the starting point for a progression of design moves that led Wild to an impeccably executed catalog to accompany the retrospective. The final book design placed Kippenberger's work within the time it was created but also reflected the present moment when it was being examined.

To reflect the unassuming design of the books, Wild chose the typeface Walbaum, knowing that not only

would it look beautiful in her intended two columns, but also that its elegance had great potential to set off the energetic images of Kippenberger's artworks.

Instead of resizing his horizontal images, Kippenberger would simply tip them sideways to fit the size of his books. In a nod to the artist, Wild did the same in her book design, rotating not only images but also some of the text. Even though designing a book that requires reading both vertically and horizontally is something she normally avoids, it seemed like a very fitting, 'elegiac,' tribute to Kippenberger. Wild framed a few of the pages with black borders, intensifying this homage.

Kippenberger often sketched on hotel stationery, and the centered script in the logos at the tops of these drawings sparked Wild's imagination. To capture both the spirit of his life and the spirit of the time of the exhibition, she chose Monotype Script in bold for the title of the book and centered it for smaller subheads and running heads on the shoulder to contrast with the two-column Walbaum.

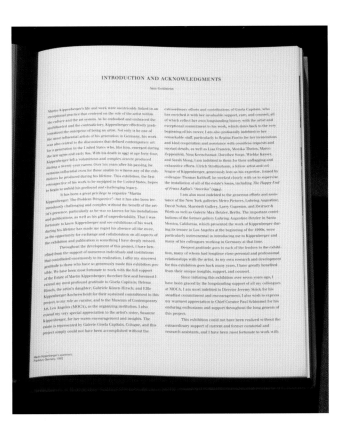

'I'm not that interested in being a historicist; I'm more interested in being of the time, making something reflect the moment and the circumstances of its design.'

For the Kippenberger catalog, Wild created a simple two-column grid, with text set in Walbaum.

Rotated pages echo a technique that Kippenberger used in his own book layouts.

Above: Horizontal and vertical rotation was used throughout the catalog, including in the typesetting. In this interview, initials are rotated ninety degrees.

Below: In the spirit of Kippenberger's own book layouts, Wild rotated some images to fit the catalog pages.

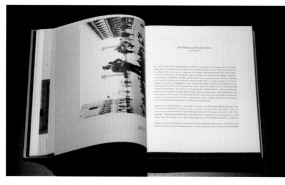

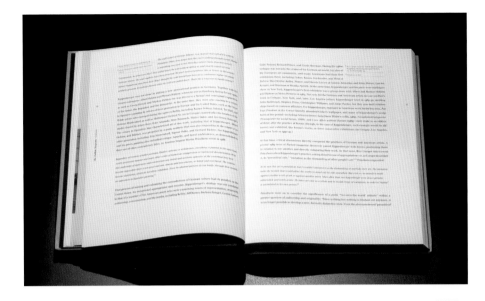

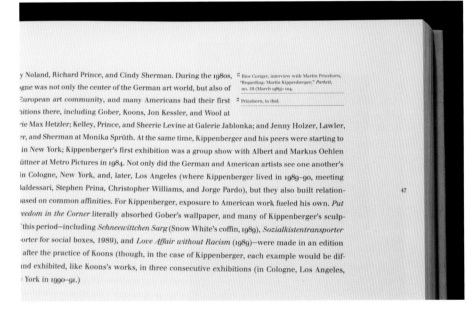

Above: Small footnotes were nested into the text column rather than inserted at the bottom of the page. Footnote numbers were turned sideways to further embed the idea of rotation.

Creative DNA
Lorraine Wild

Lorraine Wild is a designer and writer, and has taught at the California Institute of the Arts (CalArts) since 1985. She received a BFA in Design from Cranbrook Academy of Art in 1975. While working for Vignelli Associates in New York from 1977 to 1978, she began her research on the history of American graphic design, which led to her graduate studies at Yale University, culminating in an MFA in 1982.

Wild remembers wandering through the huge assortment of books in Yale's Sterling Library, as well as the stacks at Cranbrook, and being struck by books that reflected their moment in time. This experience drives her continuing pursuit of design history.

Feeding her brain has always been part of her process, and her brain has in turn fed other designers with some of the most intelligent writing about design, published in magazines including *Emigre*, *Eye*, and *ID* and in books and anthologies such as *Looking Closer: Critical Writings on Graphic Design* and *Graphic Design in America: A Visual Language History*.

Wild was a founding member of Studio ReVerb in 1991. In 1996 she left ReVerb and started Green Dragon Office, where she currently works with associate Ching Wang. Her work has been widely exhibited and she has received many honors, including the AIGA medal in 2006.

Me Company

Virtual Models

'Without the narrative, you are not
doing your homework.'

While on assignment in 1955, David Douglas Duncan, the prominent
Life magazine photographer and war correspondent, was given a small
first-century stone engraved with what appeared to be a rooster's head.
It reminded Duncan of the work of a more contemporary artist—Pablo
Picasso. Duncan presented Picasso with the stone, mounted in a ring set-
ting, as a gift; Picasso's first remark was, 'I wonder what tool he used?'

Today, the same question may be asked when encountering the work of Me
Company, headed by Paul White and Jess Warren. Their imaginary compositions merge the recognizable with the fantastic to tell stories that both
stimulate viewers' imaginations and express their clients' messages for the
music and fashion industries.

Narrative is always the starting point for their work. The process begins
with an original script, a poem, or a myth. They are open to serendipity, but
start with what White refers to as a 'serious plan.' A great deal of time is
spent up front to create a rough story line and a collection of ideas that
can be used to 'flesh out' the forms as they progress through the project.
'Without the narrative,' White says, 'you are not doing your homework.'

Once the primary visual grammar is established, White and Warren then
fine-tune it in relation to the narrative. No preliminary sketches are done
on paper, but virtual iterations are progressively generated on the computer
and discarded. 'Sometimes you need to turn the thought process off,' says
White. 'Notions of composition come best when there is scant regard
for outcomes.'

An, the main character in Me
Company's advertising campaign
for fashion house Kenzo's Autumn/
Winter 2001 collection.

Facing page: The computer-
generated garden landscape in
which the narrative of An and her
lost brother, Stan, plays out. The
scenery has a surreal complexity
that incorporates unexpected
shifts of form, color, and scale.

The computer-generated structures behind their work are at once architectural and organic: fluid, in flux, and morphing. The first step is a wire model
generated by Warren using Autodesk's three-dimensional modeling program Softimage. Warren describes the computer as a lens—a view through
a porthole. Both Warren and White feel that this technology gives designers a new way of seeing, one that doesn't exist in the real world. 'The
strength of the computer is that it lets you see in a nonlinear way.' Its ability
to add complexity and create an unusual sense of space is unsurpassed.
Seeing the software as a doorway through which the narrative emerges is
key to generating their highly imaginative imagery.

After the architectonic space is created, color, texture, and lighting effects
are brought into the composition by White. The final assembly relies on
a perceived tension between the mapped space and the randomness of
more fluid surface treatments. These poetic forms emanate a kind of optical
music through color values and harmonics. The entire composition is a
journey through virtual models representing three-dimensional spaces and
objects, but presented two-dimensionally.

This symbiosis of narrative and technology, under the strong influence
of natural forms, underpins the elastic reality of Me Company's imagery.
'Nature is the best model,' says White.

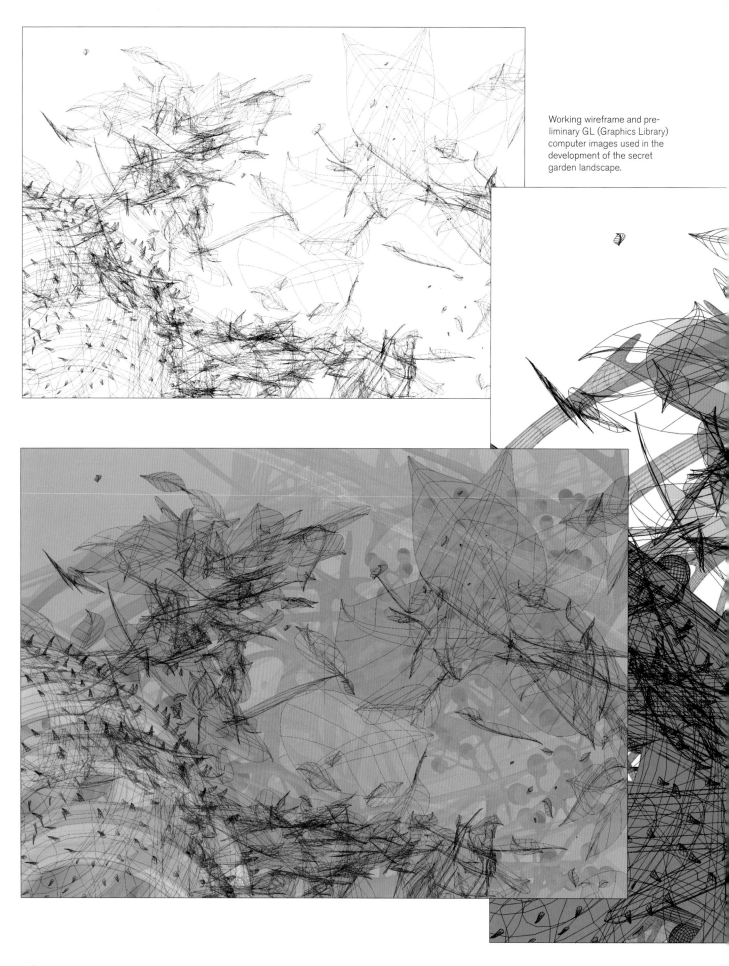

Working wireframe and preliminary GL (Graphics Library)
computer images used in the
development of the secret
garden landscape.

'The strength of the computer is that it lets you see in a non-linear way.'

Final image of the garden after colors and textures are added.

'This kind of love offered a certain intimacy and longing.'

Throughout the process one thing becomes evident: research is essential in order to make such complex imagery. This encompasses both the clients' project parameters as well as the world of ideas. To that end, the Me Company studio maintains an immense library containing the work of photographers, painters, sculptors, and architects, as well as mythology, classics, and fiction. Visible on their shelves are books on Zaha Hadid, Victor Vasarely, Karl Blossfeldt, Kenzo Tange, and David Bailey. They explain that they can spend one day looking at Brutalist architecture and the next day looking at organic 'pods' designed by Tange. Victorian ornament, sacred geometry, or even Eclecticism can spark ideas.

One of Me Company's projects was an advertising campaign for the Autumn/Winter 2001 collection of the fashion house Kenzo, titled 'An and Stan.' The narrative for the sequence of images was conceived as a story of melancholy and loss, a sister remembering a brother who is no longer alive. 'This kind of love offered a certain intimacy and longing,' says White. While the story was initially based on grief, it culminated in the joyful reunion of the siblings within a magical garden.

The visual process started with a carefully orchestrated photographic session. Shots of the female model for An were taken from multiple angles and poses, in anticipation of the compositions that would be necessary to complete the sequence. The lost brother, Stan, was carefully constructed from the images of female An. Crafting a believable face for Stan turned out to be more difficult than White and Warren had imagined, because of the built-in tendency in humans to recognize faces based on extremely minute subtleties. In addition, they had to anticipate the different lighting that would be required in each frame of the story.

The 'magic garden' that is the scene of An and Stan's reunion was constructed first with individual floriated geometries and then rendered in layers. This build technique allowed for the overlapping of multiple plantlike structures, in varying colors and textures, to form a dense forest of natural forms. To complete the surreal fantasy, a sense of motion, created by a combination of limited focus and multiple repeated elements was layered into the compositions. Once this elaborately blended backdrop was combined, the separately constructed images of both An and Stan were strategically placed.

The figures appear at ease within this imaginary garden, emerging seamlessly from the organic forms. We are the visitors, allowed only discreet glimpses of this inventive world and then left to wonder at the true nature of it. As did Picasso when first viewing the first-century stone etching, we wonder what tool they used.

These finished images were generated from a narrative where nature and dreams become one.

Facing page: An enters the secret garden longing for her deceased brother, Stan.

These images demonstrate the degree of effort Me Company go to in order to ensure that the narrative they have imagined will be interpreted successfully by their audience.

Left: The character of Stan was created from photographs of the model who posed for An.

Below: Close-up of Stan. The realistic level of detail in the face, including the addition of facial hair, was critical in supporting a convincing narrative.

Right: Combined image of An and Stan prior to being placed in the garden.

Below: An and Stan as they appeared in the final image of the narrative, set within the landscape.

An as she explores the garden.

Creative DNA
Me Company

Paul White set up Me Company in 1985. The design group began working primarily for the music industry, forming an early and lasting relationship with the performer Björk. Over the years, the list of clients has expanded to include Nike, Kenzo, Ford, and Lancôme—each seeking Me Company's unique point of view.

For the past twelve years White has worked in partnership with Jess Warren, who started out as a sculptor and model maker—an important prerequisite for the wire models he now generates using computer software.

White and Warren both insist that, regardless of any preconceived concepts the client may have, the first rule of the studio is to please themselves and remain true to their principles.

Me Company continues to explore the relationship between narrative, art, fashion, music, and the infinite possibilities of advanced three-dimensional computer technologies. White says, 'There is no such thing as a normal production process. Every project is different and needs a unique and different treatment.'

Facing page, top left and right: The elements in the vegetation change as Stan appears in the garden.

Facing page, bottom: As An and Stan are joyously reunited, the plants become even more colorful and activated, echoing the emotions of the characters.

abstraction

5 Abstraction

Abstract symbols have always been part of visual communication. Throughout time, inventive form-makers have been challenged to produce symbols that express complex ideas. These graphic images, often developed to mediate temporary issues, sometimes through a series of steps, evolve into permanent modes of understanding.

Distilling an idea requires a great deal of effort. As the designer works to condense a concept by employing or creating specific symbolic or iconic representations, additional, related issues, may surface and threaten to transform the meaning of the attempted design. The designer must therefore be thoroughly prepared, through extensive research, to recognize and express only those meanings most closely aligned with the core of the concept.

Graphic design, as the word 'graphic' implies, demands a vivid, clear sense of form-making. Being able to create concise meaning using a restricted grammar requires

focus and determination, as well as an understanding that the more reduced a design is, the more demand will be placed on every gesture within the final symbol. It is this action of visual reduction in order to achieve universally accessible meaning that truly challenges the skill of the designer.

The abstract commissions that follow are by Korean designer Ahn Sang-Soo, Swiss designer Ralph Schraivogel, and US designer Michael Bierut. Each case study reveals a unique story and an individual approach to solving abstract graphic design challenges. 'Symbol' looks at Ahn's meditative and introspective approach to designing a new peace symbol. In 'Type as Image,' we see Schraivogel's generative and exhaustive exploration of every possible variation until the final form was resolved. 'Identity' examines Michael Bierut's close collaboration with his client and steady reflection at each stage of the process of creating a logo for the New World Symphony.

Ahn Sang-Soo

Symbol

The twentieth century's peace sign was created in 1958 by London textile designer Gerald Holtom for a nuclear disarmament march.[1] At that time the world's ambition for peace was focused on ending war and stopping the proliferation of nuclear weapons. Holtom's now-familiar design was a simple circle with lines diagramming two semaphore flag signals: two arms down for *N* and one arm up for *D,* which stood for 'nuclear disarmament.'

Fast-forward to 2004, when Life Peace Organization, a foundation dedicated to the harmonious coexistence of all living things, commissioned Ahn Sang-Soo to design a symbol for a new Korean peace movement. This assignment required conceptual thinking on a high level in order to both define and represent 'peace' in the twenty-first century. Ahn described the process as long and contemplative—one that took many months of concentration and sketching. He considered many key precedents of abstraction as he worked on the problem. One principal image that influenced his idea was Indra's net, an ancient Indian metaphor that symbolizes the interconnections among all living things. The net is visualized with a jewel at each intersection, with every jewel representing a piece of nature; all the jewels are identical, indicating that all parts of nature are equally significant, and each jewel reflects all the others, so that a change in one jewel is reflected in all.

'In the twenty-first century, with the cold war behind us, the focus of the peace movement has shifted from fear of war to advocating for sustainability and honoring the interconnection of all living things.'

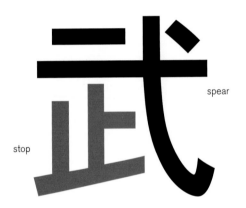

spear

stop

military power

woman

baby son

good

Recognizing the complexity of the message he needed to communicate, Ahn brainstormed ways to support a hierarchy among the various parts of the representation. He looked at the Chinese writing system because of its compact distillation of meaning. In explaining the power of the condensed iconography of the characters, Ahn cites some examples: 'Good,' he says, is represented by the symbol for 'baby son' next to the symbol for 'woman.' He goes on to explain how the arrangement of the parts can further convey meaning. For example, the character for 'military power' combines the characters for 'spear' and 'stop' and thus represents power not as the aggressor, but as the force to stop the aggressor.

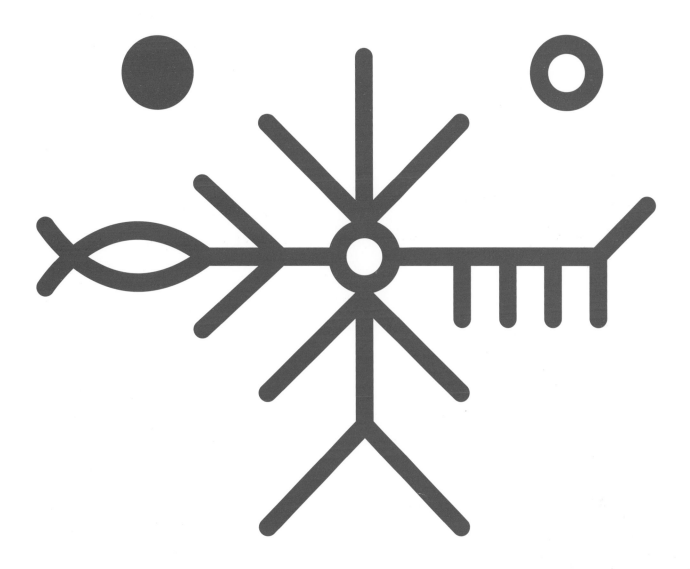

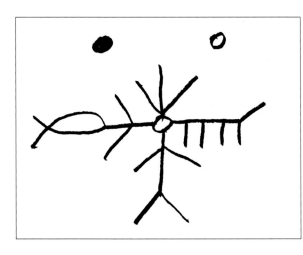

Above: Ahn's final symbol links all living things together. The two circles at the top, one solid and one outlined, represent the sun and the moon. Around the central circle below rotate icons for four-legged creatures (right), humans (bottom), fish and birds (left), and plants (top).

Left: One of Ahn's initial sketches for the symbol.

'You heighten your awareness about
the connections, but it takes time.'

Ahn was also reminded that Russian filmmaker Sergei
Eisenstein acknowledged in his diaries that Chinese
writing had informed his breakthrough idea of montage,
the sequencing of symbolic images to convey meaning. In Eisenstein's 1925 film *Battleship Potemkin*, the
famous Odessa battle scene captures the chaos and
terror of the situation through rapid editing cuts—a pair of
broken glasses, a baby carriage rolling down a staircase,
glimpses of facial expressions—rather than a conventional
battle scene, allowing the audience to participate in the
moment through the act of assembling the discrete parts
in their mind's eye.

Perhaps the most profound inspiration during the process
of developing the peace symbol was Ahn's recollection
of a traditional early morning ceremony at a Buddhist
temple. The ritual, an 'awakening ceremony', consists of
four highly symbolic ten-minute parts. First, the monks call
the sky to awaken by striking a large metal 'cloud' with
a mallet. In the second part of the sequence, the monks
pound on a large fish-shaped drum to wake all the sea
creatures. Next, the beating of an oversized calfskin drum
awakens the four-legged creatures. The final phase of the
ceremony is the ringing of a giant bell that is struck by
swinging a large log suspended by ropes from a wooden
frame to wake the humans.

Slowing down the process was critical in order to build
his analysis of 'peace'; there was no alternative but to spend
an extended period of time reflecting on the problem and
letting his thoughts connect. 'You heighten your awareness about the connections,' Ahn says, 'but it takes time.'

After many months of analysis, Ahn established the
iconography for the peace sign as well as the arrangement of the various components. His final holistic design
is formed around a central circle with man at the bottom,
four-legged creatures on the right, fish and birds to the
left, and plants at the top. Two circles above, one solid
and one in outline, depict the sun and the moon. He is
gratified that people have remarked that it resembles a
petroglyph because that is exactly the level of timeless
abstraction he was looking for. The symbol also carries
traces of the visual language he has developed over
the years for his Korean Hangul typeface designs. 'One
project extends your thinking into another,' he asserts.

Facing page: Ahn renders the symbol using brush and ink.

Left: Ahn signing a large brush-and-ink version of the symbol.

Ahn's 1991 *Bomb Fishes* poster is an example of his continued interest in developing a reductive visual grammar that symbolizes highly abstract, complex meanings.

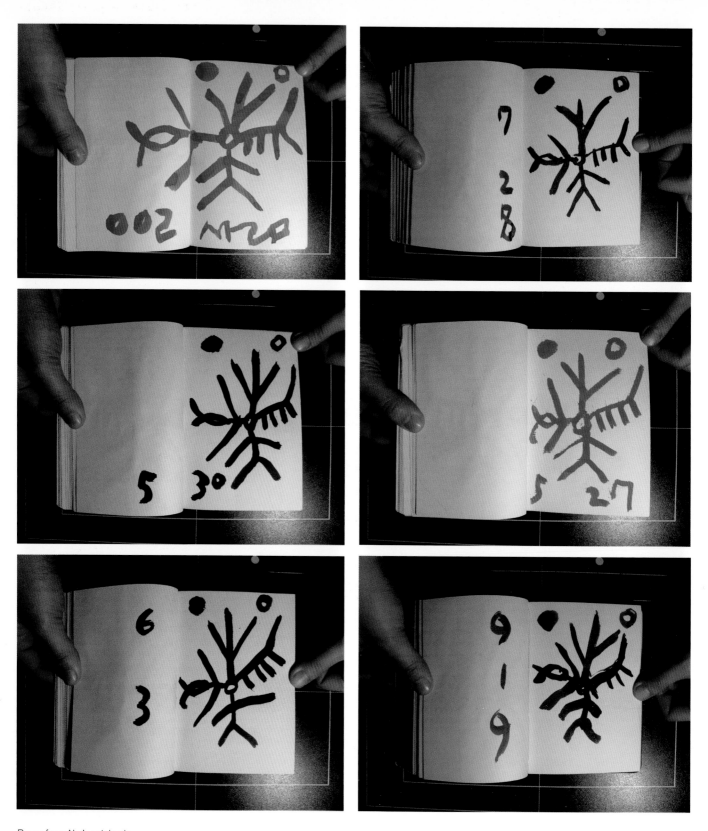

Pages from Ahn's notebook
showing examples of his daily
renderings of the symbol.

Dan Boyarski of Carnegie
Mellon University's School of
Design renders the symbol
during a visit to Ahn's studio.

When the design was finished, Ahn extended its agency
as a living expression by encouraging others to draw
and interpret it. He wants the mark to 'grow' as other
people translate it. Ahn redraws the symbol each day
and keeps a journal in his studio where every visitor is
invited to create a version.

Creative DNA
Ahn Sang-Soo

In 1983, Ahn Sang-Soo was
named Designer of the Year
by *Design* magazine; in 2004,
Idea magazine declared him
the most innovative designer
in contemporary Korea.

Ahn is the founder of Ahn
Graphics, a design firm and
multimedia, advertising, and
publishing house. He obtained
his BFA and MFA in 1981 from
Hongik University in Seoul,
where he has taught typography
since 1991. He received his PhD
in 1996 from Hanyang University
in Seoul and was awarded an
honorary design doctorate in
2001 by Kingston University,
London.

After college, Ahn worked for
an advertising agency for five
years; from 1981 to 1985 he was
also an art director for *Madang*
and *Meot* magazines. Since
1998, he has been the editor and
art director of the underground
art-culture magazine *Bogoseo/
Bogoseo (Report/Report)*. Ahn
served as the 1999–2001 vice
president of Icograda, the
International Council of Graphic
Design Associations, and was
the chairman of the Icograda
Millennium Congress 'Oullim
2000' in Seoul. He also chaired
the organizing committee of
TypoJanchi, the first biennale of
Korean typography in 2001.

Ahn has been awarded many
prizes and accolades for his
work, including the 1998 Grand
Prix at Zgraf 8 (the International
Exhibition of Graphic Design
and Visual Communication) and
the 2007 Gutenberg Award by
the City of Leipzig, Germany, for
his services to the advancement
of book arts. He is best known,
however, for his typographical
contributions to the Korean
Hangul language.

1. Melissa Breyer, 'Where did the peace sign come from?'
http://shine.yahoo.com/event/green/where-did-the-peace-
sign-come-from-2392559

Ralph Schraivogel

Type as Image

Designing a poster to embody Edmund Burke's saying 'Evil prevails when good men fail to act' was by no means a common assignment for designer Ralph Schraivogel. The idea came from his long-time client and friend Sacha Wigdorovits, an entrepreneur and public relations advisor with many of Schraivogel's posters on his office walls.

Wigdorovits heard Chancellor of Germany Angela Merkel in 2008 at a ceremony commemorating the fiftieth anniversary of Kristallnacht (Night of Broken Glass). Merkel spoke of the majority of Germans at that time in history not having the courage to protest against the barbarism of National Socialism; a few minutes later, Wigdorovits called Schraivogel with the idea to make Burke's quote into a poster.

Schraivogel was a bit apprehensive about the idea, believing the written words were so moving that he could make no further improvement to them, but ultimately agreed to go ahead with the project under the condition that there would be no deadline: if he thought of nothing he would be obliged to do nothing and in that case there would be no charge. Both were determined that the poster would also not be sold or used commercially.

'I always try everything even if I know it's nothing.'

prevails when good men fail to **Evil** **act**

EVIL PREVAILS WHEN GOOD MEN FAIL TO ACT

Schraivogel's design process for the poster began with a series of computer-generated typographic explorations. Typefaces, sizes, weights, and arrangements were logically played out in a sequence of variations. Both upper- and lowercase letters were tried in many combinations. Shown here is a representational selection from hundreds.

EVIL
PREVAILS
WHEN

GOOD
MEN FAIL
TO ACT

The insertion of a line
transforms the quotation
into an equation.

Dramatic perspective makes
'Evil' more menacing.

The contrasting scale of
the words teases out a
secondary message.

Scale shifts among the words
create both a rhythm and
sense of progression.

Schraivogel experimented for some months before he presented an idea to Wigdorovits. He described his process as 'engineering,' in that it progressed methodically through a logical sequence of configurations to explore the potential for expression embedded in the quotation. Schraivogel's aptitude for logic and math is evident in his painstaking testing of as many typeface sizes and weights, and relationships among the words, as he could possibly generate, so that the chance of a correlation—a place where the idea and the design hit the mark as an abstraction—was as high as possible.

Eventually some typographic arrangements began to take shape as images, including a bomb, a human body, and DNA. While some variations had the potential to make striking posters, Schraivogel rejected them because they presented too limited a viewpoint.

Over the course of a few months, Wigdorovits and Schraivogel met to look at ideas. Wigdorovits remembers, 'These encounters were extremely fascinating and enriching for me because I learned a lot about Ralph's thinking… at the same time we had very fruitful discussions about the topic of the poster.'

Hundreds of sketches later, the two words 'evil' and 'live' appeared as a mirrored pair from a pile of printouts on Schraivogel's desk. He remembers noticing the combination while he was talking on the telephone. He then called Wigdorovits and explained the idea. They were both very excited, but that was just the beginning. Schraivogel used Adobe Illustrator to generate every conceivable combination of potential relationships and inversions of the words in an effort to 'make sure that nothing was left unconsidered.'

Stacked configurations of the words and syllables of the quotation began to form some iconic shapes: DNA, a human body, and a bomb.

EVIL
PRE-
VAILS
WHEN
GOOD
MEN
FAIL
TO
ACT

EVIL
PRE-
VAILS
WHEN
GOOD
MEN
FAIL
TO
ACT

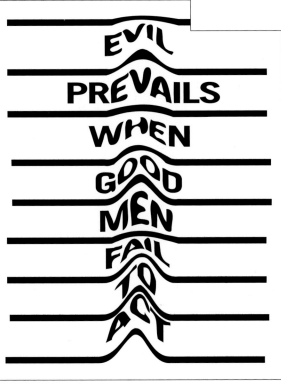

Variations on the bomb's proportions and a study of type radiating from a red circle to suggest a target.

Schraivogel considers the experience of working with the computer after many years of manual work to be very visual: 'You can try everything and you tend to spend even more time in the process—that forces you to think more.'

EVIL
PRE-
VAILS
WHEN
GOOD
MEN
FAIL
TO
ACT

Left: The type distorted to look like a flag over a dead body.

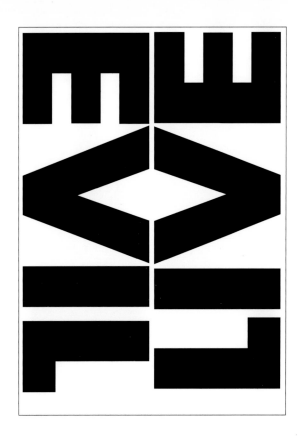

"The world is a dangerous place to live, not because of the people who are evil, but because of the people who don't do anything about it." Albert Einstein

Evil prevails when good men fail to act

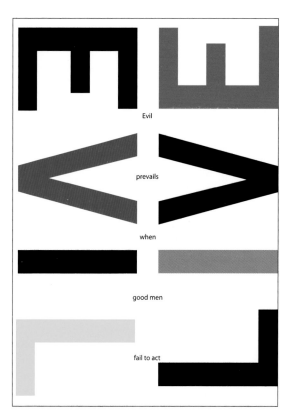

Evil

prevails

when

good men

fail to act

Above: The breakthrough moment where the pairing of the two opposite words was discovered. Once the idea was conceived, it was pushed to the maximum. Schraivogel wanted to 'do something impossible with it.'

Schraivogel revisited all his previous experiments with type—upper- and lowercase, and various color applications—in light of the new concept.

He concluded that while the combination of the upward and downward reading was visually interesting, it was not strengthening the idea.

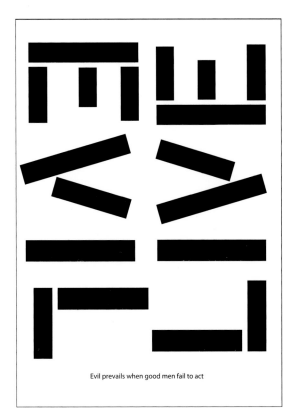

Evil prevails when good men fail to act

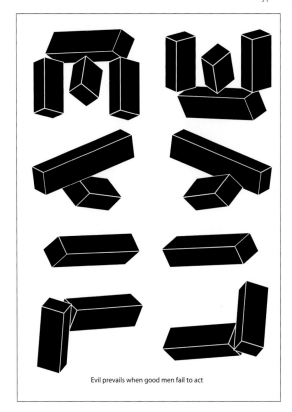

Evil prevails when good men fail to act

A matrix of letters showing angles of rotation in increments of ten degrees.

'You always go back to what you tried before and try it again at each phase.'

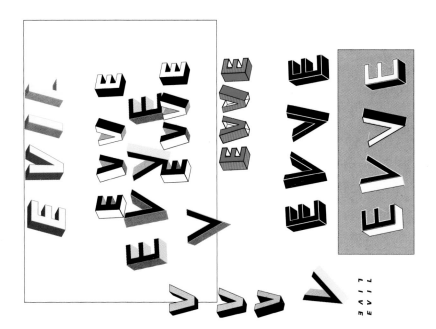

Three-dimensional letterforms opened up the potential for multiple readings.

Schraivogel experimented with both rotation and dimension to test further possibilities.

121

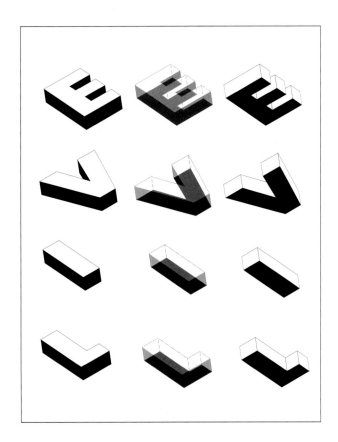
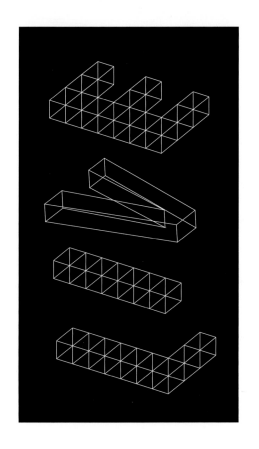

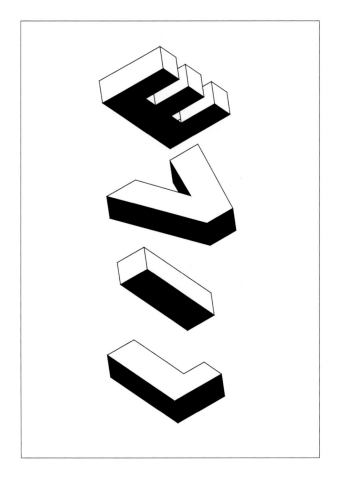

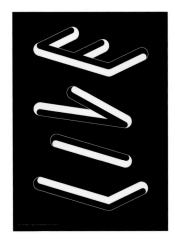

1.2

Experimentation and careful analysis of the structure of the three-dimensional letterforms led to the discovery that only one set of letters was necessary to embody both words.

Schraivogel meticulously tested various proportions and relationships among the letters, looking for the right balance between tension and legibility.

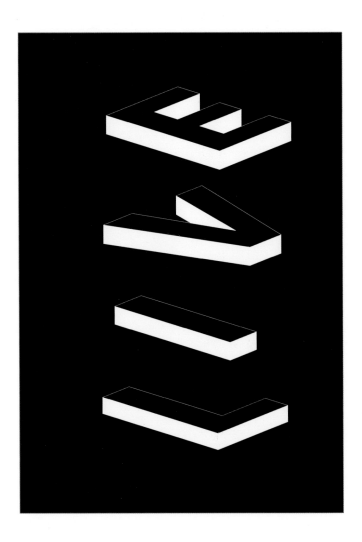

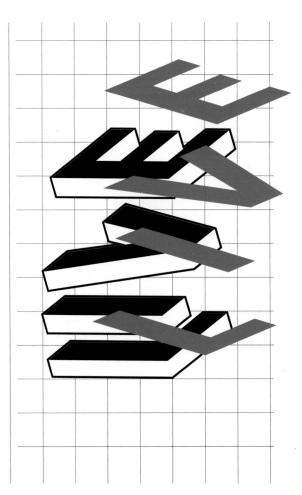

During the final phase of the design process, Schraivogel focused on refining the expression of the suspended typographic sculpture. Through trial and error, he found the optimal letter shape, line weight, and perspective for the text. The subtle variations in the outlining of the letters can only be appreciated upon close examination.

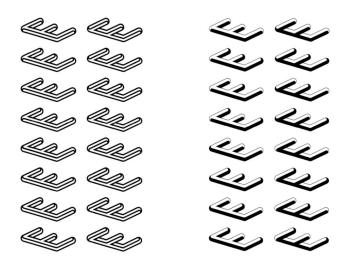

Schraivogel eventually decided on a single three-dimensional interpretation encompassing both words, reading 'evil' from top to bottom and 'live' from bottom to top. He describes the final composition as a suspended typographic sculpture. Its floating presence embodies the intangible abstraction of the quotation.

Both Schraivogel and Wigdorovits agreed that black and white was the ultimate color choice for the message. The white letters against the black background strengthened the optical play between the two words, rendering a stark contrast between 'live' and 'evil'. This was reinforced by Wigdorovits's conviction that 'there are no shades of gray when you are dealing with evil'. The picture plane became a poetic construction of the quotation as the white of the paper illuminated the word 'live', glimmering in the expansive darkness.

Once the poster was complete, Wigdorovits wrote an extended dedication, *Against Forgetfulness and Apathy*, summarizing his thoughts. The essay explains his motivations for commissioning the poster:

The question thus remains. What do I intend to achieve with this 'LIVE–EVIL' poster?

On the one hand, I wanted to create a work which I can offer as a sign of gratitude and respect to those whose energy and commitment in fighting evil I have found both impressive and moving. On the other hand, this poster should also serve as a daily reminder to me of my duty not to look the other way or stay silent when injustice occurs.

Finally, I hope that this poster, wherever it may hang, will jolt at least some of those who see it from the dangerous and indifferent trance into which our society seems to be drifting.

If it can achieve that, then 'LIVE–evil prevails when good men fail to act' will have already fulfilled its purpose.

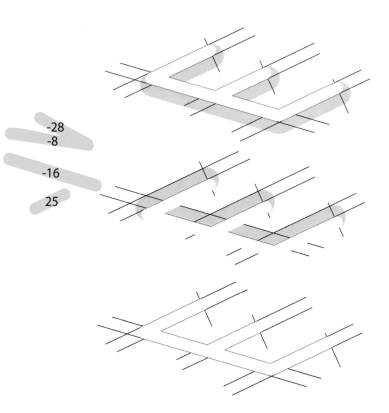

Above: Study of corner angles and radii.

Facing page: Schraivogel's final design succeeds in fully embodying the quotation 'Evil prevails when good men fail to act'.

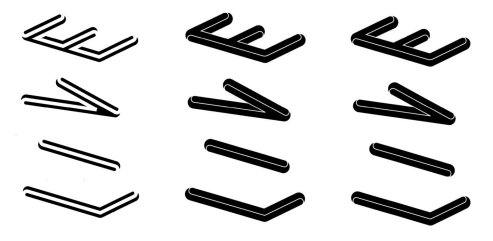

Creative DNA
Ralph Schraivogel

Ralph Schraivogel was born in 1960 in Lucerne, Switzerland. Even before he reached kindergarten, he knew he liked painting and drawing. Among his heroes as a young child were Rembrandt and the Impressionists. His passion was copying the style of other artists. When Schraivogel was a student, there were no academic fine arts programs in Switzerland, just applied art, so he studied graphic design at the Schule für Gestaltung Zürich from 1977 to 1982.

Schraivogel then opened a studio in Zurich. He designs publications, logos, and corporate identities, but his passion is creating posters for cultural events. He has designed posters and program magazines for the Zurich repertory cinema Filmpodium since 1983 and posters and exhibition announcements for the Museum für Gestaltung Zürich since 1984. He has also designed posters for the African film festival CinemAfrica since 1989.

Schraivogel has received the Swiss Federal Prize for Applied Art three times, as well as major prizes in poster festivals and biennials throughout the world. International solo exhibitions have brought his work to a wide audience, and his posters are included in numerous collections around the world, including that of the Museum of Modern Art, New York.

Schraivogel has taught at the Hochschule für Gestaltung und Kunst Zürich and has been a guest professor in Berlin at the Universität der Künste. He currently teaches at the Hochschule Luzern and the Schule für Gestaltung Basel.

Michael Bierut

Identity

In Michael Bierut's identity for the New World Symphony, abstraction allows a simultaneous representation of both the objective and subjective aspects of the organization. Finding the perfect solution for this challenging project required an extraordinary degree of honesty and persistence.

'I think certain kinds of identity projects require completely different kinds of processes.'

Bierut explains: 'I've never made a brief saying we will show you five things and reduce it to two things and then one.' 'Instead,' he tells his clients, 'we're going to go on an adventure together and at the end of it we'll have something everyone will like.' He says, 'It takes passion and commitment and really listening very actively to the person who knows the thing that you are trying to represent, and who will be living with the thing you give them.'

The initial visual concept for Bierut's New World Symphony logo was a typographic abstraction of Gehry's New World Center.

The New World Symphony was founded in the late 1980s by conductor Michael Tilson Thomas as an orchestral academy for outstanding graduates of music schools from all over the world. Once accepted, the musicians become fellows and are immersed in orchestral training and performance. The new identity was commissioned in tandem with the academy's move into the New World Center, a twenty-first-century state-of-the-art performance center in Miami Beach designed by architect Frank Gehry.

At first glance, the building is surprisingly rectilinear. With the exception of a few organic flourishes that burst out of the top, the signature Gehry forms are harnessed within the building and delineate the various functions inside. Gehry's structure incorporates technology such as media displays for concerts and video collaborations for distance learning with international guest conductors. The flat exterior walls double as projection screens that are used for live-feed concerts and free movies to engage the public in an adjacent 2.5 acre park, designed by the Dutch architectural firm West 8.

Pentagram, the design firm at which Bierut is a partner, was commissioned to design both the identity and the signage system. Bierut explains that Gehry's architecture mapped the space so well that there wasn't a need for an elaborate wayfinding system. However, the process of working with Michael Tilson Thomas and Executive Vice President Victoria Rogers on the signage project informed an in-depth understanding of the distinctive attributes of the institution that fed into the identity design.

Bierut worked in collaboration with designer Yve Ludwig on the identity. As the two began brainstorming, they faced many challenges. Three words and five syllables added up to a lot of letters to pull together, and even though it would have been easier to design something around the initials *NWS*, they had not heard anyone use the initialism and abandoned it as a direction at first.

Their first proposal was a typographic abstraction of the Gehry building. Simple rectangles formed a graphic framework of solids and voids for the letterforms to push against, echoing the architect's concept of using irregular walls to define interior spaces. They further experimented with Gehry-like forms by bending the design and were excited that it was so malleable, keeping its identity in a seemingly infinite number of variations.

Bierut remembers that even though this was his first idea, at the time he thought he had 'nailed it.' However, the clients thought the design was somewhat over-worked and busy. 'Just because you've solved every element of the problem,' he observes, 'it doesn't mean the result is good.'

'When they're looking at the thing, they're not looking at the brief, they're not looking at the rationale, they're not looking at a particular set of problems that have to be solved, they're just looking at something, and having this immediate visceral reaction.'

Above: Scale model of Frank Gehry's design for the New World Center.

Right: Experiments with the first design concept, reflecting the contours of Gehry's building. The design expressed the directives for the identity, but the client found it overworked.

As Bierut explains his process, it is obvious that his intelligence and tenacity work hand in hand. He embraces a give and take with his clients and relies on their input to figure out what is and what is not working, and to motivate the next stage of the process.

For the next round, the designers focused on the contrast of old and new, thinking about a twenty-first-century center in which eighteenth-century music is played on old instruments, some of which haven't changed since the Renaissance. They condensed this historical comparison into a typographic expression using the typeface Requiem, designed by Jonathan Hoefler and based on handwritten capitals from a sixteenth-century writing manual, in combination with the minimalist geometric typeface Futura, designed by Paul Renner in the early twentieth century. The name 'New World Symphony' naturally justified onto two

lines and was, in Bierut's words, 'appealingly unaggressive like a signature—simple and confident.'

As a second direction, they abstracted the *N*, *W*, and *S* into the kind of forms that Gehry had designed in the building and tested various combinations to see if they could make the forms appear musical. Michael Tilson Thomas responded very positively to this design idea but thought it was too heavy and asked to see some more spontaneous, organic iterations.

Bierut experimented with brushstrokes for an afternoon but, in the end, wasn't satisfied with the direction they were taking. He sensed he was losing direction; in order to become grounded in the process, he had the idea to ask Thomas what kinds of visual suggestions he had given Gehry at the beginning of the design process for the building.

N W

abcdefghijklmnopqrstuvwxyz
ABCDEFGHIJKLM
NOPQRSTUVWXYZ
1234567890

Requiem, designed by
Jonathan Hoefler in 1992.

abcdefghijklmnopqrstuvwxyz
ABCDEFGHIJKLM
NOPQRSTUVWXYZ
1234567890

Futura, designed by
Paul Renner in 1927.

NEWWORLD SYMPHONY

This variation of the logo alternated old and new typefaces to reflect the contrast and harmony between the twenty-first-century building and the classical music played inside.

'Every designer who gets to a certain level always has those things that always work; you have to both embrace them and fight them. If you fight them you won't grow because you have to acknowledge where you've been before.'

Studies of the initial letters of the symphony's name as simple curved forms.

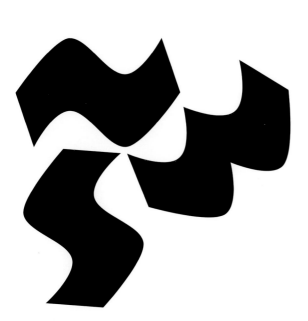

The designers tried rotating the abstract letters around a middle point to create unity and dynamic counterforms.

In response to the client's feeling that the first rendering needed more spontaneity, Bierut experimented with brushstrokes.

The primary image Thomas had shown Gehry as he developed the concept for the building was Kurt Schwitters's *Merzbau*, an improvised construction that Schwitters gradually installed in the interior of his family's house in Hannover. Thomas had used it as an example of how planar surfaces can be used to articulate the spaces between them. This discussion of positive and negative space prompted the next idea for the identity: a simple black square with bleeding letterforms that converged to form a cropped monogram. The angular *N* and *W* were not easy to merge with the curvilinear *S* but the insertion of photographs into the negative spaces helped to enliven the mark, and when repeated it generated lively patterns. In the end, however, Bierut sensed it was too corporate looking and lacked the musical quality that seemed to be eluding them.

Thomas sent Bierut a page of his own sketches. Taking the gesture seriously but not wanting to succumb to a refinement of the client's idea, Bierut, who usually uses his notebooks for more perfunctory notations, filled the pages of his notebook with calligraphic initials done in a similar spirit but in a tighter graphic way.

Kurt Schwitters, *Merzbau*, photographed in 1933.

A new concept inspired by Schwitters's *Merzbau*, one of the visual suggestions given to Gehry at the beginning of the design process for the New World Center.

'Graphic designers know exactly what's happening here,' jokes Bierut, 'but in my heart of hearts I knew it was too corporate looking.'

Thomas sent a page of sketches of his own monogram concept to Bierut for inspiration.

'I was looking for the language and images that motivated the building, thinking that if I could get back to that starting point that would give me some clues....Instead of "he briefs Frank, he designs a building, I look at a building, and I do this," what if we both started from the same place?'

Taking Thomas's sketches as a starting point, Bierut made dozens of calligraphic monograms in his notebook.

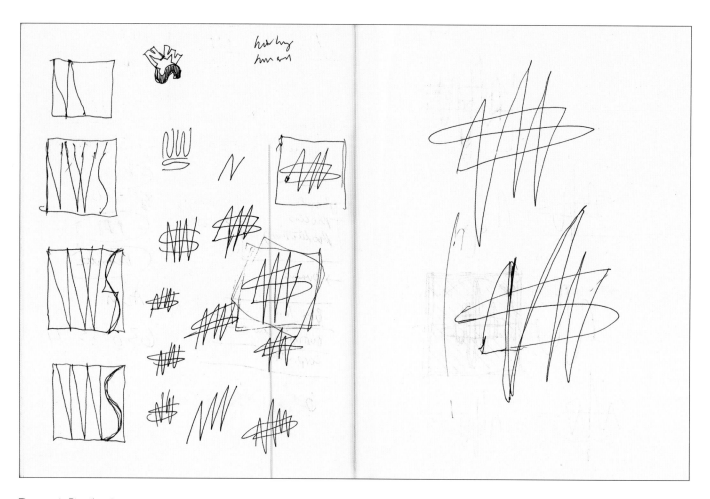

The page in Bierut's notebook where the final design
idea surfaced.

Below, left to right: The
logic behind the design was
presented to the client in the
form of a 'design equation.'

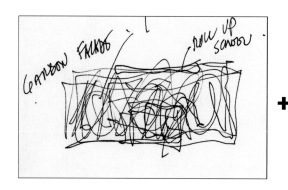

One of Gehry's sketches for
the New World Center, showing a containing shape with
forms bursting out of it.

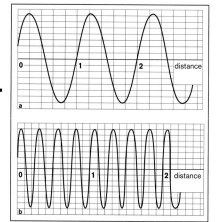

Oscillating waves showing
frequency and pitch, reflecting
the technological aspects
of music.

A textbook of basic
conducting techniques.

Sketch locating the intersections of the curves embedded in the form.

'I keep a notebook with me all the time. It's not a sketchbook brimming with ideas. I don't draw, I make notes from meetings and annotate ideas as quickly as possible with as little refinement as possible.'

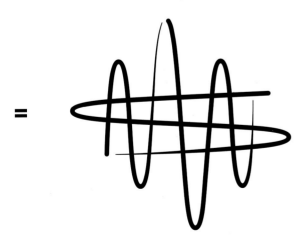

Final mark.

There is a passionate excitement in Bierut's voice as he leafs through the notebook, recounting his process and finally landing on the page where the breakthrough took place. He had made a holistic flourish—one continuous line that incorporated the three letters, beginning with the *N* and *W* as a horizontal wave that was crossed by the *S*, resulting in a beautiful biaxial symmetry.

Bierut further refined the mark with Yve Ludwig, pushing for perfect harmony and regularity among the curves and proportions. They recognized that, after this long process, they had designed something with abstract characteristics that both provoked a visceral reaction and provided an intellectual context.

'When I look at what we ended up with, it was what was being asked for all along.'

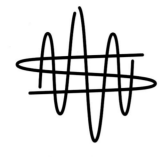
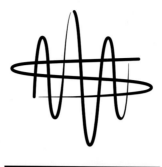
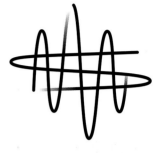

Testing ways to interrupt the flow of the line to define the letters *N*, *W*, *S* using a simple gap, tapering line weight, and tone.

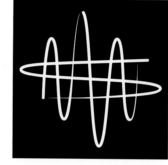
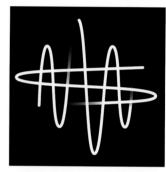

Same variations as above, but reversed out of a black field.

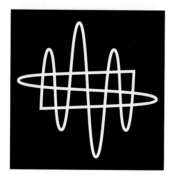
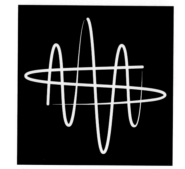
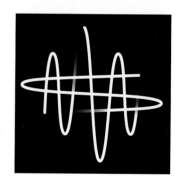

Various ways of starting and ending the *S*—some open-ended and some closed.

To reinforce his instincts with logic, Bierut presented the concept as sequence of images that outlined his and Ludwig's thought process and defined the abstract characteristics of the logo. The sequence for the presentation was illustrated as an equation: one of Gehry's original sketches for the New World Center, plus oscillating sound waves, plus conducting gestures, equals the final mark.

Once the initial configuration was determined, there were still many rounds of refinement made by the designers to balance the gestural qualities of the mark with legibility. Bierut explains: 'Some decoding was desirable but it was also important to have a somewhat immediate reading

of the *N*, *W*, *S*.' Varying the weights of the strokes aided readability while at the same time giving the logo a more organic quality, which related to the gesture of conducting.

After all the hours of work, the resulting mark looked almost effortless. Bierut acknowledges, 'It felt like a human hand had slashed in the air and made this thing.' Reflecting on his process, he concludes, 'I don't have a model process and much of what I described is nothing more or less than the interaction we had with the source material and the client we worked with.' He also stresses the importance of being sensitive to both when and how to present stages of work to clients, to allow enough time for the process to comfortably unfold.

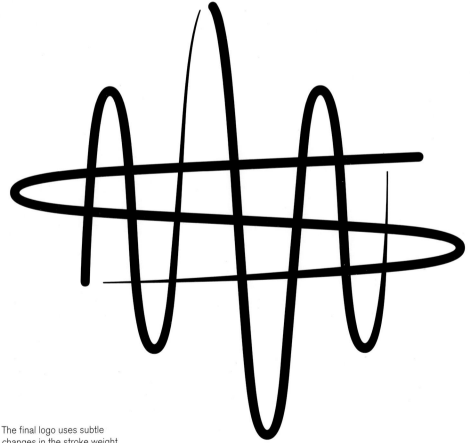

To engage the public, the logo needed to be strong enough to be applied to consumer collectibles.

The final logo uses subtle changes in the stroke weight and small spaces between the letters to support readability. The *S* overhangs the beginning of the stroke but stops short of closing the shape.

Creative DNA
Michael Bierut

Michael Bierut grew up in Cleveland, Ohio. At around age eight, remembers his father pointing out the hidden pictorial meaning in the Clark forklift company logo as they passed it on the highway—the *L* in 'Clark' lifting the *A* like a forklift.

Bierut studied graphic design at the University of Cincinnati's College of Design, Architecture, Art, and Planning, graduating summa cum laude in 1980. Prior to joining Pentagram in 1990 as a partner in the firm's New York office, he worked for ten years at Vignelli Associates, ultimately as Vice President of Graphic Design.

At Pentagram, Bierut has created identities, packaging, publications, and environments for such clients as the Brooklyn Academy of Music, Harley-Davidson, Saks Fifth Avenue, Princeton University, the *New York Times*, and the William Jefferson Clinton Foundation. His work has ranged from brand standards to signage to design consulting.

Bierut was president of the American Institute of Graphic Arts (AIGA) from 1998 to 2001. He was elected to the Art Directors Club Hall of Fame in 2003 and received the AIGA Medal in 2006. He is a senior critic in graphic design at the Yale School of Art, coeditor of the anthology series *Looking Closer: Critical Writings on Graphic Design*, and a cofounder of the blog DesignObserver.com.

6.1 Iteration

Philippe Apeloig, Paris

6.2 Systems

Anette Lenz, Paris

Vincent Perrottet, Paris

6 Development

Once a design concept is established, the development phase begins with rapid prototyping. This is an invigorating activity as well as a critical juncture for any project. At this stage, even though it is clear in the designer's mind, the idea is still very fragile. There is a constant possibility that the designer may overwork the project to the point where the spark of imagination in the original idea is lost.

It is correspondingly important to be receptive to new options as the work progresses. The designers we interviewed have a fluidity and an openness in their process such that they may complete stages A, B, and C, but if idea F shows up, they will run with it.[1] They also track each stage of their work as the process unfolds, so that if they reach a point where they have gone too far in any direction they can go back a step or two. Each project builds a further consciousness of their process and sparks ideas and methods that cross over into the next one.

This chapter contains two case studies centered around the theme of development. 'Iteration' looks at Philippe Apeloig's process of incremental refinement during the development of two poster projects. 'Systems,' illustrated by the work of Anette Lenz and Vincent Perrottet, shows how concept development can be extended into intricate systems that link a series of designs internally as well as externally to their contexts and audiences.

---

1. Interview with Michael Johnson, February 2009.

6.1

Philippe Apeloig

Iteration

'Before I start to design I need to be inspired by something I see, something I smell, something I taste.'

The graphic design process is a constant exchange between uninhibited experimentation and careful judgment. Designers have various ways of facilitating a quick—ideally, uninterrupted—feedback loop between imagination and analysis. The computer's facility for quick iteration supports the development of an idea, allowing a designer to begin with one design configuration and then progressively build other arrangements.

Design perfectionist Philippe Apeloig embraces the extent of the computer's capacity for variation, and works back and forth between printouts and the screen—drawing, annotating, and then further refining. The computer is never a starting point for him, but it is where he pulls his ideas together.

Much of his inspiration comes from living in the city of Paris, observing both its complexity and its culture. For a poster announcing the 2009 Fête du livre, Aix-en-Provence's annual literature festival, focusing that year on Asian writing, Apeloig began by assembling a palette of images exploring his impression of Asian urban space. The surreal planar space of Michael Wolf's photographic series *Architecture of Density*, with its images of the facades of multistory buildings—expansive yet cropped—sparked Apeloig's imagination; he also explored more atmospheric ideas of Asia as paradise, represented by flowers, colors, and silk. Apeloig was fascinated by the contrast between the tourist perspective and the astonishing reality of living in crowded, polluted cities and focused on bringing that to light in the design of the poster. 'There's no space to breathe, that's the idea.'

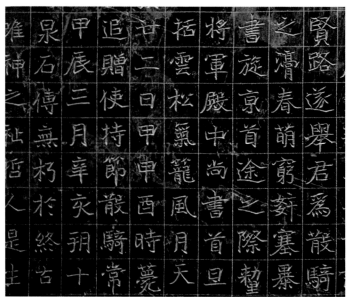

The multistory building facades of Hong Kong, captured by Michael Wolf in his *Architecture of Density* series, were a strong influence on Apeloig's poster for the 2009 Aix-en-Provence literature festival, which focused on Asian writing that year.

Apeloig also researched other visual material that would connote Asia: the colors of flowers and silks and examples of Asian calligraphy.

The finished poster for the
2009 Aix-en-Provence
literature festival.

Apeloig began working with the title of the festival, trying to incorporate in the typography the various urban forms that were taking shape in his mind. The computer allowed him to make endless adjustments. After hundreds of iterations testing sizes, weights, and scale variations, he got to a point where the complexity of the type was overpowering the initial concept. As much as Apeloig loved the energy and rhythm in the type, he realized that in order to define the facade of a building it would be necessary to have more uniformity in the letters.

The final poster beautifully reflects in both its typography and its colors the multiplicity and the literature of Asia: an extreme urban landscape touched by tropical flowers and silk.

Keeping his research images in mind, Apeloig turned to the computer and began to synthesize, making hundreds of typographic variations,

testing sizes, weights, and combinations. Focusing on the concept of urban landscape, he constructed an abstract facade with the type.

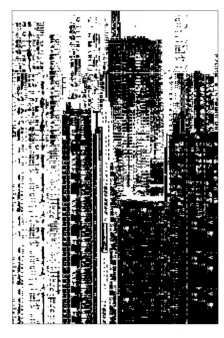

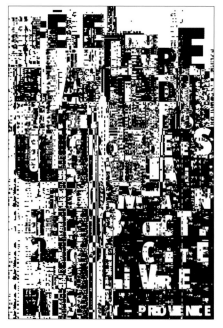

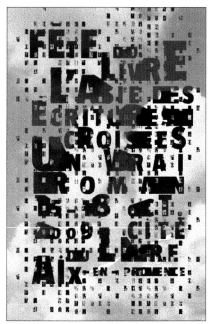

As interesting as the typographic compositions were, Apeloig realized they were costing him the uniformity

that had been at the core of his original idea; the complexity of type sizes was compromising the poster's legibility.

Tropical flowers were the source of inspiration for the color schemes.

'There's no space to breathe,
that's the idea.'

The final poster was also printed
in a second color scheme, lighter
and less saturated.

In 2007, the Aix-en-Provence literature festival celebrated Wole Soyinka, the Nobel Prize–winning Nigerian writer whose inspiration is drawn from his life experiences in various cultures and whose literature illuminates many opposing concepts of home and the world. Soyinka's roots are in the Yoruba tribe, which has a strong cultural foundation in arts and crafts. In his poster for the festival, *Wole Soyinka: La maison et le monde*, Apeloig used weaving, one of the Yoruba's most expressive craft forms, as a metaphor for the array of themes that Soyinka intertwines in his written works.

In thinking about the poster as a woven object, Apeloig began with an archetypal portrait of Soyinka, cut it into strips, and literally wove it back into a cohesive characterization of the author. He made many paper mock-ups using different-sized strips, narrow and thick, perpendicular to the picture plane and angled, exploring color, scale, and rhythm; he then stepped back to evaluate the results. Too much rhythm began to imply that Soyinka was a musician; type began to play a critical role in establishing the poster as a portrait of a writer. In signature style, Apeloig customized the typeface, adding a strong horizontal connecting bar that strengthened its direction, making it act as weft and warp to fuse the type and image.

Apeloig began developing his idea by laser printing an image of Soyinka in different colors. He then cut the prints into strips of various sizes and wove them together.

Above and facing page: Experiments using cut-paper strips.

Variations in strip color, width, rhythm, progression, and orientation were investigated.

Apeloig's final poster for the
2007 Aix-en-Provence literature festival, celebrating the
Nobel Prize–winning Nigerian
writer Wole Soyinka, was
woven from two photographic
images with different levels of
orange saturation.

The final prototypes show how Apeloig pushed to weave the typography into the image. The introduction of horizontal crossbars to the letterforms reinforced the direction of the type as an integral part of the woven portrait. Apeloig almost always customizes his type to make it more malleable.

Creative DNA
Philippe Apeloig

Philippe Apeloig grew up in Paris and was educated at the Ecole supérieure des arts appliqués and the Ecole nationale supérieure des arts décoratifs. After graduating and spending two transformative training periods at Total Design in Amsterdam, he worked as a designer for the Musée d'Orsay in Paris from 1985 to 1987.

In 1988, Apeloig received a grant from the French Foreign Ministry to work in Los Angeles with designer April Greiman. In 1993–94, he was honored with a research and residency grant at the French Academy of Art in the Villa Medici in Rome.

Apeloig taught typography and graphic design at the Ecole nationale supérieure des arts décoratifs in Paris from 1992 to 1999 and at the Cooper Union School of Art in New York from 1999 to 2002.

Apeloig established his own design studio in Paris in 1989 and now creates posters, logos, typefaces, and communication materials for cultural events, publishers, and institutions.

In his youth Apeloig trained for a career in dance, a form he now looks back on as 'moving paintings.' This influence is evident in the way he choreographs type. He thinks of type as a means to interpret a text in much the same way that dancers and actors do; he sees the poster as a 'stage' and considers both the performance and the poster to be ephemeral. Type in motion is something Apeloig has a natural affinity for and he often creates animations to complement his poster and identity projects.

6.2

Anette Lenz and Vincent Perrottet

Systems

Visual systems in graphic design operate on many levels and are embedded in both design products and design processes. The innovative use of systems can build both visual and conceptual associations that focus meaning. An elegant graphic design system acts as a unifying structure as well as a platform from which multiple iterations can be developed. Once set in motion, an intelligent visual construct takes on a life of its own and can lead to endless invention as its form and variations are explored.

Paris designer Anette Lenz has tremendous facility for inventing visual and conceptual design systems. Her poster for the exhibition *Mois du Graphisme* (Month of Graphic Design), a traveling show that took place in the mountains of Echirolles, France, demonstrates how multiple symbols can be condensed into one iconic image. Lenz selected the letter *M* as the primary visual symbol, because it represented the words 'mois' (month), 'maison' (museum or house), and 'mont' (mountain); at the same time, she recognized that its shape reflected both the slope of a rooftop and the peak of a mountain. The resulting design—a singular folding letter, rendered with light and shadow against a light blue field—evokes the image of an isolated structure within a landscape.

Lenz also used an inventive visual system to connect an event to its location in her poster promoting a film festival at the La Géode Omnimax cinema in Paris. Lenz translated the striking spherical architecture of the cinema into the central graphic element for the poster. The design's geometry and bright spectrum of color activated the walls of the underground Métro stations with an unmistakable graphic image that passing viewers immediately associated with La Géode.

'There is always a ping-pong between the hand and the head. It's an exciting process, and while you're doing it you discover relationships that you wouldn't have thought of before.'

Lenz chose the typeface for her La Geode poster based on its similarity to the type used in Paris Métro station signage.

Right: The spherical form of the La Géode Omnimax cinema itself was the starting point for the poster design.

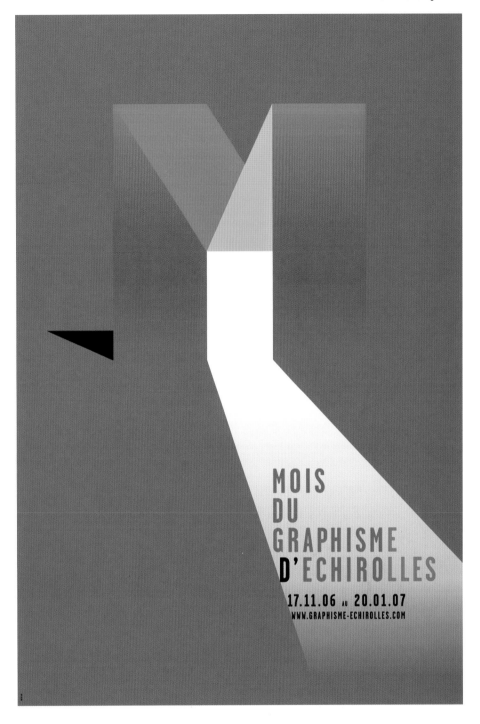

Lenz's poster for *Mois du Graphisme* (Month of Graphic Design), a traveling exhibition that took place in the mountains of Echirolles, France.

A white wedge, like light emanating from a doorway, leads the viewer's eye to the *M* and emphasizes the title of the exhibition.

Acknowledging the exhibition's focus on female designers, Lenz highlighted, in red, the *e* in 'Graphisme' and *lles* in 'Echirolles'—spelling 'elles' (women).

The subliminal relationship between the shape of the letter *M* and the mountain peaks is amplified when the poster is seen in its final context.

What is remarkable about Lenz's process is how holistic it is in its approach, conceptually fusing time, place, and subject. Lenz is a master at both understanding and executing complex structures. Not only does she consider the dynamics at work within each component of a design—be it a poster, invitation, or brochure—she also understands the context in which the design will be delivered. All of these parts cohere into a whole as she assembles a poetic order among them.

Striking examples of this are the promotional campaigns she has produced for Paris's Théâtre de Rungis, whose annual season of eighteen performances include music, dance, comedy, and drama. Knowing that the primary context of the promotional posters would be the corridors of Paris Métro stations, she focused on the large signboard spaces (39 $3/8$ x 59 $1/16$ in.; 100 x 150 cm) and exploited their potential as a vehicle for telling a quiet story in a noisy location.

Thinking about theater as an abstracted space, and inspired by Josef Albers's *Homage to the Square* series, she made a composition in two mirrored halves. On the left, she positioned a pink rectangle against a magenta field; on the right, she mirrored the composition with a gold rectangle against white. These simple boxes acted

as a 'stage' and defined what was 'in front' and what was 'behind the scenes.' The compositional elements, which could change shape and size from poster to poster, became the framework for bold diagrammatic collages that metaphorically represented key ideas in the performances. She found the system to be tight but also versatile, something she needed in order to produce multiple pieces for the season within both a short time frame and a fixed printing budget.

The brochures for the plays employed the same symmetrical design, with progressively darker shades of gold ink—another embedded system that symbolized the passing of the season's performances. Lenz acknowledges that some of these moves are deeply subjective and that most viewers won't notice them, but they are still important to her.

'It would be pretentious to say you had all the parts of a design in your mind from the beginning. But you have one or two points in your mind, and it takes off from there.'

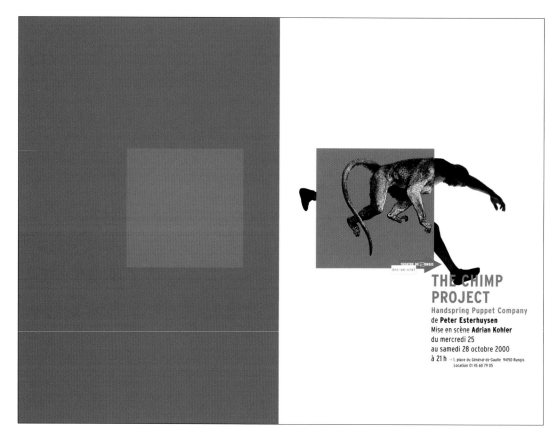

Lenz's versatile system of mirrored rectangles allowed her to explore the notion of theater as abstracted space, adjusting the compositional elements to express the core themes of each play in the Théâtre de Rungis season.

The first design Lenz used to test the creative potential of her rectangle system was the poster for *The Chimp Project*, the story of a monkey who mistook himself for a human.

THE CHIMP PROJECT
Handspring Puppet Company
de **Peter Esterhuysen**
Mise en scène **Adrian Kohler**
du mercredi 25
au samedi 28 octobre 2000
à 21 h → 1, place du Général-de-Gaulle 94150 Rungis
Location 01 45 60 79 05

Facing page, top: One of Lenz's posters in its final context, the Paris Métro.

Facing page, top inset: All the designs with their various proportions were overlapped for a simultaneous reading to promote the complete season in one poster.

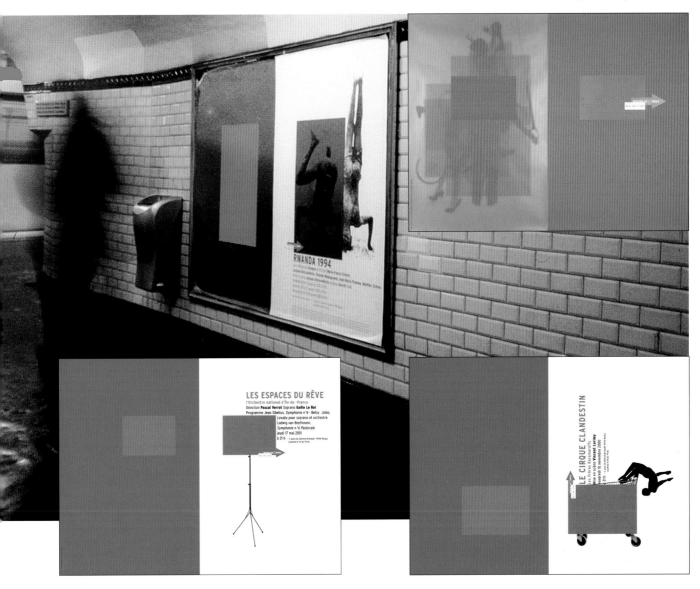

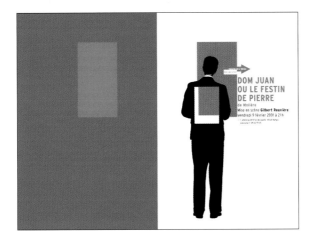

For a classical music concert, the music stand was used to represent the 'stage'.

This poster represents the story of two Russian circus jugglers who escape in a container to Paris.

Here the rectangles of Lenz's design system operate as both mirror and void to portray Don Juan as simultaneously narcissistic and empty.

The religious hypocrisy of the protagonist of *Tartuffe* is indicated by the simple juxtaposition of a provocative photograph and a cross.

'I always need those subtle little things in a design.... It's like a Hitchcock film: you see it three times and each time you discover another layer.'

Beginning in 2001, the city of Angoulême invited Anette Lenz and Vincent Perrottet to design the materials for the annual summer festival of the Théâtre d'Angoulême. Looking for an influence within the elaborate urban landscape that would guide them in structuring their project, Lenz and Perrottet found Angoulême permeated by various forms of art. Attracted to the arrangement of windows on the newly restored theater itself, they transposed the facade of the building into a grid system for their campaign. This system could be reproportioned and color-coded to represent different aspects of the performances: blue for dance, violet for theater, pink for variety, and yellow-green for music.

Angoulême is also home to the Musée de la bande dessinée (Comic Strip Museum) and each year hosts the Festival international de la bande dessinée d'Angoulême (Angoulême International Comics Festival). The theme of comics is visible throughout the city, with large cartoon murals on buildings and street signs shaped like speech bubbles. This cultural feature found its way into Lenz and Perrottet's design system as well: they used photographs and text in comics-style panels to construct behind-the-scenes stories of the performance companies involved in the festival.

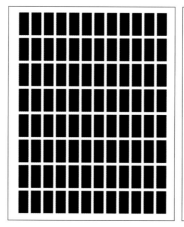
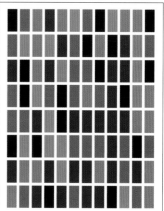

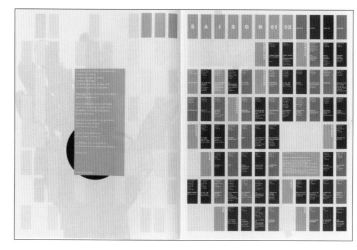

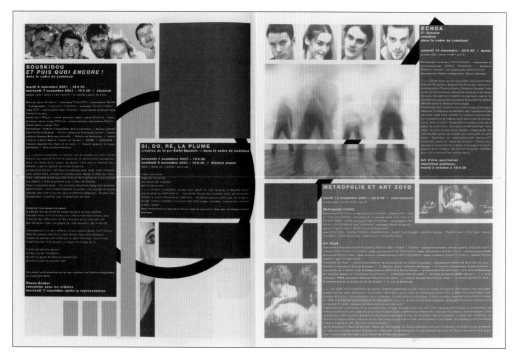

For the 2001 Théâtre d'Angoulême promotional materials, Lenz and Perrottet looked to the city itself for inspiration. They developed a flexible grid system based on the facade of the theater and also incorporating other art forms celebrated in the city, such as comics, reflected in the panels of photographs and text.

Color halftones facilitated the use of many images regardless of their original resolution.

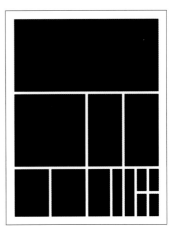

Above: The facade of the Théâtre d'Angoulême inspired the grid system that underpinned Lenz and Perrottet's poster designs.

Below: The posters were color coded: blue for dance, violet for theater, pink for variety, and yellow-green for music. The black elements were glossy.

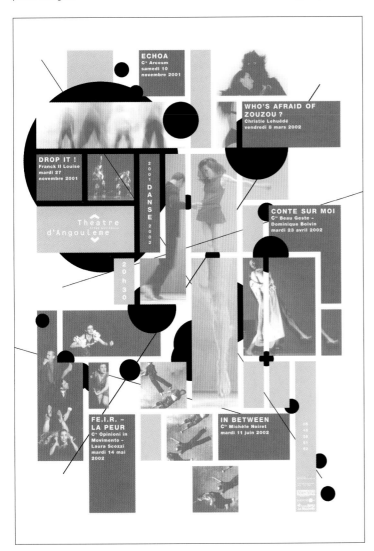

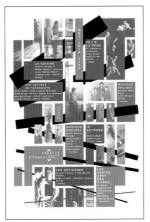

Lenz and Perrottet brought in photographer Myr Muratet to generate images for the 2002–3 Théâtre d'Angoulême program. Muratet spent two weeks photographing the Angoulême landscape for the project.

In 2002 the designers invited French photographer Myr Muratet to interpret Angoulême, intending to use his images in the program for the 2002–3 Théâtre d'Angoulême season. The very act of photographing the city became a kind of theater—a play of the real people and an expression of itself. Muratet spent two weeks photographing the town and its environs. While viewing the resulting images on a table, the designers noticed an interesting relationship between a photograph of a swimmer diving into the lake and another landscape image. The froth on the surface of the dark water beneath the swimmer in one photo began to react with the sky over the lake's horizon and resembled a field of stars. Attracted to this ambiguity, the designers took the water even further out of context by cropping it into an irregular shape. This exaggerated the perspective and made the gesture of the diver even more dramatic. By stacking the images and sandwiching the typographic elements between them, the designers brought the landscape closer and closer to a constructed imaginary space, like a stage.

For the interior pages of the program, the designers experimented with various arrangements of the photographs.

The juxtaposition of two pictures automatically revealed a narrative. The graphic elements extended the symbolism of the stage, even on the text spreads.

As Lenz describes: 'The graphic design became the stage, and the photographs became the story.'

'You can't tell if he's jumping into the sky or if he's diving into a new season.'

For the cover of the program, Lenz and Perrottet stacked the cropped images, layering the typographic elements between them. The landscape became more and more like an imaginary space, like a stage. They exaggerated the perspective of the landscape by reframing the photograph of the diver in a parallelogram, thus removing the surface of the water from its original context.

Creative DNA
Anette Lenz
Vincent Perrottet

After studying visual communication in Munich, Anette Lenz moved to Paris in 1990 and joined the design collective Grapus. Later, as a cofounder of Nous Travaillons Ensemble, she became involved in designing books, posters, and identities for cities and cultural institutions. Since starting her own studio in 1993, Lenz has continued working in the social and cultural field, for clients such as the City of Paris, the Ministry of Culture, Radio France, the French Senate, Museé des arts décoratifs, and the Théâtre d'Angoulême.

Lenz's numerous prizes, include the Grand Prix at the 2006 Golden Bee, Biennial Moscow, and the Silver Award at the 2007 China International Poster Biennial, Hangzhou. The posters she and Perrottet designed for the Théâtre d'Angoulême received the Silver Medal at the Tehran Biennale in 2004 and the Grand Prix at Ningbo, China, in 2004. Lenz participates in international workshops, conferences, and juries and is a professor at the Haute Ecole d'art et de Design, University of Geneva.

Vincent Perrottet was born in Saint-Denis and now works near Paris. He joined Grapus in 1983, while finishing his studies in the video and film department at the Ecole nationale supérieure des arts décoratifs. After leaving Grapus in 1989 Perrottet cofounded the studio Les Graphistes Associés and, shortly thereafter, formed the group Ne Pas Plier.

He is now an independent designer producing identities, publications, and posters for cultural, public, and social institutions, often in association with Lenz. He was the artistic director of the International Poster and Graphic Arts Festival in Chaumont from 2002 to 2009. Perrottet has also taught at the Ecole supérieure d'art et de design d'Amiens (ESAD) and Ecole d'art du Havre.

collaboration

7.1 Programming
Ben Fry, Boston

7.2 Print Production
Leonardo Sonnoli, Rimini

7.3 Title Sequence
Stephen Fuller, New York
Ahmet Ahmet, Los Angeles

7 Collaboration

Design by its very nature is collaborative. Collaboration is evident in almost every case study we have presented so far—the designers working closely with partners, clients, curators, and fabricators. It is the end product that is the important thing, not the individual egos involved. Successful teams honor each member's area of expertise and work together to craft the best solution.

For collaboration to be successful, it is also critical to find the right partnerships. This means staying connected to your design community and networking with the people who support it, such as printers and programmers. Knowing where to find the best resources is essential for any design project. This section focuses on these extended partnerships and how they broaden the creative potential of a designer's work. The 'Programming,' 'Print Production,' and 'Title Sequence' case studies illustrate how the potential of the graphic design process can be accelerated through tight alliances.

In the early twenty-first century, the computer itself has become the designer's primary collaborator. To extend

the computer from tool to participant, many designers have embraced its capacity to program design scenarios. The case study on Ben Fry looks at the software called Processing that he developed in collaboration with Casey Reas and showcases some of the ways designers have employed this program to produce new kinds of design work.

Before the days of desktop publishing, print production was always a major team effort, including typesetters, color separators, and production members who prepared the film and plates for printing. Leonardo Sonnoli's work with Corraini Editions and an offset lithographer to establish conditions for chance operations on press demonstrates that there is still room for creativity in a partnership with a printer.

Finally, the title sequence for the HBO/Playtone mini-series *The Pacific* outlines the painstaking efforts that Imaginary Forces collaborators Stephen Fuller and Ahmet Ahmet went through to design and produce a poetic work of type and image in motion.

Ben Fry

Programming

Over the past decade, computation has become a more accessible tool for graphic designers. This breakthrough has been largely facilitated by Ben Fry and Casey Reas, two programming-savvy designers who met in the Aesthetics and Computation Group at the Massachusetts Institute of Technology (MIT) in the late 1990s. They began working together while assisting their professor John Maeda with Design by Numbers, a programming language for teaching computational design. This led them to develop Processing, an environment in which to learn the fundamentals of computer programming for creative arts.

Like Design by Numbers, the aim of Processing was to make programming more designer-friendly. 'At their core, computers are processing machines,' says Fry. 'They modify, move, and combine symbols at a low level to construct higher-level representations. Our software allows people to control these actions and representations through writing their own programs. The project also focuses on the "process" of creation rather than end results. The design of the software supports and encourages sketching and the website presents fragments of projects and exposes the concepts behind finished software.'

'The idea of putting down a little bit of code, getting something up and running...it feels like a sketch.'

Facing page: Detail of Fry's *Genomic Cartography: Chromosome 21*. The work is a visual representation of the 13 million letters of genetic code that make up one quarter of the smallest human chromosome.

Below: The full-size work (8 x 8 ft; 24.38 x 24.38 m) on display at the International Center of Photography, New York, for the exhibition *How Human: Life in the Post-Genome Era*' in 2002.

Processing's workspace is a small page called a 'sketch,' similar to a blank sheet of paper. Fry explains, 'This facilitates an instant back-and-forth between the code and what it's generating, encouraging the designer to play with the code and not be precious about what they are creating.'

Fry has always been equally interested in visual art and computer science, but saw them as two separate tracks until he met John Maeda, who was visiting Carnegie Mellon where Fry was a student studying design and minoring in computer science. 'When I saw the way Maeda put design and computation together, I realized that there was another path to take with computation as a visual tool, besides interface design,' Fry says. 'I got very interested in data visualization.'

For his doctoral dissertation, titled 'Computational Information Design,' Fry chose genetics as his subject area. At the time, he explains, genetics was 'a big, messy data problem.' His work was timely, because the draft of the human genome had just been released, and the scientific developments had social and societal implications: 'We had this "book of life" but nobody understood what that meant.'

His experience with visual art drove his desire to see the data in some kind of physical form. When he heard the human genome is 3.1 billion letters long, the visual part of him wondered 'What does that mean? What do 3 billion things look like?' He started with the smallest of the human chromosomes, 50 million letters. Working with 37.5 letters per inch and a 3-pixel font, he produced an 8 x 8 foot (24.38 x 24.38 meter) printout of 13 million characters representing one quarter of the chromosome. Later for the Museum of Modern Art's show *Design and the Elastic Mind*, Fry generated a print of human chromosome 18 that covered a wall—with 72 million letters.

DESIGN AND THE ELASTIC MIND

Fry's visualization *Genomic Cartography: Chromosome 18*, 2001, on view as part of the exhibition *Design and the Elastic Mind*, Museum of Modern Art, New York, 2008.

Below: Genetic software and interface developed by Fry, which enables scientists to track changes in DNA sequences.

'If I hadn't done the printout I would have missed the details in the middle section of DNA code.'

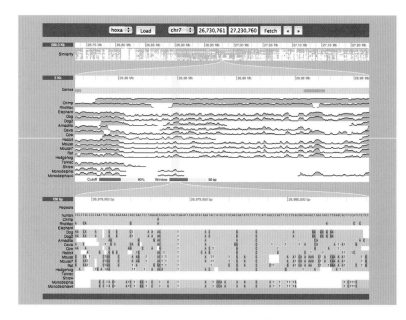

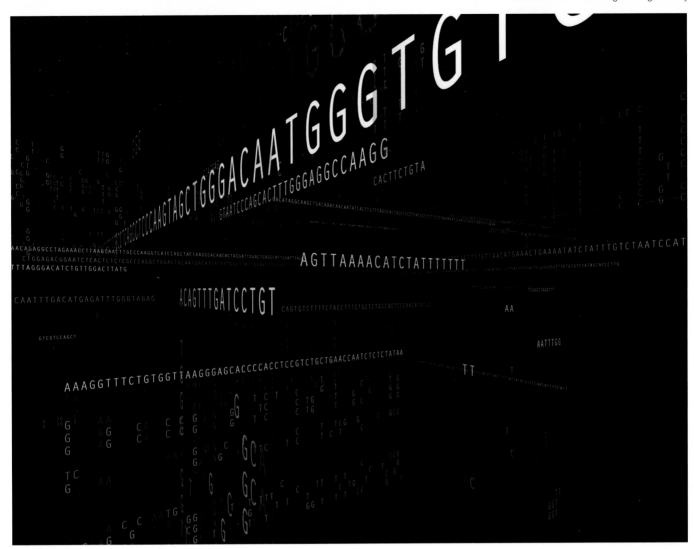

Fry's illustration *Aligning Humans and Mammals* for *Seed* magazine represents human DNA in white and that of animals in color, ordered by their evolutionary distance from humans.

Fry takes full advantage of his background in both visual design and programming, often working back and forth between looking at data physically, through models and printouts, and visualizing it with programming. Both approaches work hand-in-hand, culminating in a unique comprehension and awareness of the logical points of entry into the data.

Fry is certain that being able to look at the data sets at a large scale and seeing the patterns they generate has been a tremendous advantage when working on genetic software tools. Seeing the code in a large typographic composition has aided his understanding of the embedded relationships and has enabled him to create tools for scientists that take into consideration the importance of 'moving back and forth between the forest and the trees.'

Fry is also often asked to make data visualizations for editorial publications. He enjoys the challenge of telling a story with a data set, and the quick turnaround on these assignments—most completed within a few days—is a welcome 'antidote' to his more long-term projects.

One example is an illustration Fry created for *New York* magazine to illuminate the relationships and connections among the top fifty blogs in the world. Fry started by mapping the blogs in various ways, positioning the more connected ones closer together, and organizing them in hierarchies with the most connected at the top and the least connected at the bottom. He also experimented with how to differentiate the connections, indicating outgoing links on the left and incoming on the right.

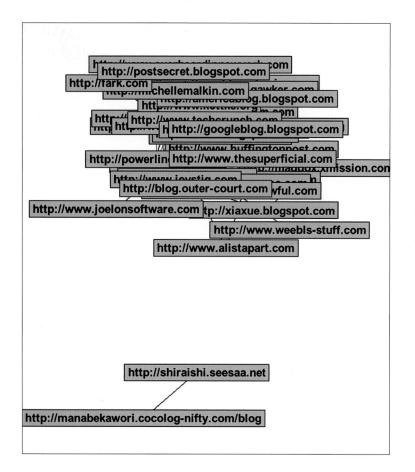

Early sketch exploring the connections among the blogs.

Frustrated with the resulting tangle, Fry stopped working with the computer and got out his sketchbook. He quickly realized that a horizontal axis was critical to orient the viewer to the map. He then decided to construct a series of arcs connecting particular points along the line of blog titles from left to right. The arcs' colors designate the type of blog: orange is technology, blue is politics, pink is gossip, and green is 'other'.

In the final illustration, levels of activity are reflected in the height of the arcs, with the highest representing the ten most popular blogs. The lines get brighter in the direction of the link. The less popular blogs all link upward, and while there is some cross-linking among the top ten, none of them link down.

Fry gets the most satisfaction from seeing what other artists and designers produce with Processing. He notes: 'The most successful users move back and forth between tools—making a program with Processing, using the output from it, and putting it back with other sets of software tools.'

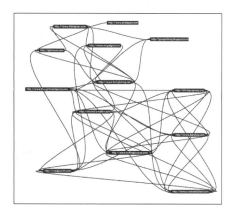

Experimentinng with grouping the various blogs to show meaningful connections among them.

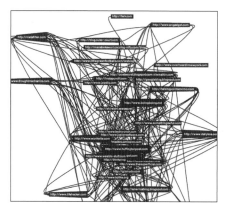

Here more connected blogs are positioned closer together.

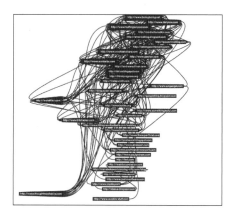

Fry tried organizing the blogs from top to bottom, from number one down to twenty-five, with incoming links on the right and outgoing links on the left. The final result was too tangled to be useful.

Top: An unexpected irregularity in the code produced an interesting image. The 'bug' caused arcs that were extended well beyond their intended locations, but Fry felt these gestures helped inform the final design.

Bottom: Fry's final illustration of the relationship between the top fifty blogs for *New York* magazine. The height of the arcs represent the popularity of the blogs, and the brightness of the lines indicates the direction of the links between them.

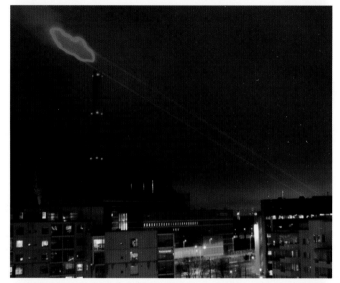

'Now that we are off the screen, this is something that everybody in the town can understand and see, whether they have a computer or not.'

'A neat idea for creators to think about is the thing they created versus what someone else created. Do they own the process or the artifact?'

A project Fry is particularly impressed with is *Nuage Vert*, a data visualization created by the Helsinki artists' group HeHe, who collaborated with a local power plant to stage a real-time installation in the city that would generate energy-conservation awareness. The group worked with a live feed of data that indicated the amount of power being generated at any given time. Then, using Processing, HeHe made a program that would output an image in the form of a green cloud shape scaled to represent the amount of power produced by the plant. The program controlled a laser that projected the cloud image into the sky, where smoke, coming from the power station, was rising into the atmosphere. This created a real-time visualization of the power—and therefore the emissions—being generated by the station. The cloud provoked a conversation and town-wide events to conserve power. The resulting change in consumption, indicated by the shrinking size of the cloud, was there for all to see.

The Helsinki artists' group HeHe used Fry's Processing program to design a cloud that represented the amount of power being generated from their local power plant. The cloud was projected into the sky to reflect off the smoke being released from the plant.

Another of Fry's favorite examples of other designers using Processing is Nervous System, a design studio founded in 2007 by Jessica Rosenkrantz, who holds degrees in biology and architecture, and Jesse Louis-Rosenberg, a mathematician and former consultant at Gehry Technologies. Using Processing, the two designed a software tool that generates organic jewelry designs based on biological structures, and even allows users to modify the designs on their website by twisting, warping, or breaking apart the embedded geometry.

Fry is fascinated by the blurring of boundaries exhibited in these and other examples. He feels that the Processing software facilitates a collaborative relationship between the user, the audience, and himself, and best represents the future creative uses for the computer.

Creative DNA
Ben Fry

Ben Fry is the principal of Fathom, a design and software consultancy located in Boston. He received his doctoral degree from the Aesthetics and Computation Group at the MIT Media Laboratory, where his research focused on combining computer science, statistics, graphic design, and data visualization as a means for understanding information. After completing his thesis, he spent time at the Eli and Edythe L. Broad Institute of MIT and Harvard, developing tools for visualizing genetic data. During the 2006–7 academic year, Fry was the Nierenberg Chair of Design for the Carnegie Mellon School of Design.

Processing, the computational design program that Fry developed with Casey Reas (University of California, Los Angeles), won a Golden Nica from the Prix Ars Electronica in 2005 and received the 2005 Interactive Design prize from the Tokyo Type Directors Club. Processing was also featured in the 2006 Cooper-Hewitt National Design Triennial. Fry and Reas have written a number of books on Processing, including *Processing: A Programming Handbook for Visual Designers and Artists* with MIT Press, and *Getting Started with Processing* with O'Reilly and *Make* magazine.

Fry's personal work was shown at the Whitney Biennial in 2002 and the Cooper-Hewitt National Design Triennial in 2003. Other pieces appeared in the Museum of Modern Art in New York in 2001 and 2008; at Ars Electronica in Linz, Austria, in 2000, 2002, and 2005; and in the films *Minority Report* and *The Hulk*. His information graphics have illustrated articles for *Nature*, *New York* magazine, the *New York Times*, *Seed*, and *Communications of the ACM*.

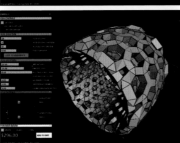
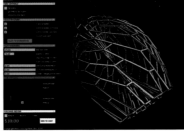

Above: An interactive application, designed using Processing, on the Nervous System website allows customers to create and modify jewelry designs based on subdividing cells.

Left: A ring from Nervous System, created by combining Processing with 3-D printing technology.

7.2

Leonardo Sonnoli

Print Production

Before the introduction of desktop publishing, printing was a collaborative effort among a team of experts who worked closely at every phase of the project—from selecting paper to final press decisions—to insure that the results were both technically and aesthetically pleasing. Today the designer works autonomously preparing the artwork and interacts with the printer on a limited basis.

Keeping precise control of each phase of a design project is the objective of most designers. On occasion, 'happy accidents' occur within the process and are recognized as improvements on the original intended result. Often designers respond to such aberrations with the desire to bring the project 'back in line.'

However, when Leonardo Sonnoli, working with Irene Bacchi, was called upon by the publisher Corraini Editions to create a new sixteen-page promotional publication, he decided to let the idea of the random accident drive the entire project. The project is given to a different designer each time it's published, with no restrictions on content, so each designer is driven to create something fresh. The idea is to promote Corraini Editions as a creative and artistically vital company.

Sonnoli found inspiration in his days as a young designer working for an office that produced posters for a local supermarket; the posters used graduated colors, and were later overprinted with specific price and merchandise information. The printer, he recalled, had, under the direction of the poster designer, used a technique known at the time as 'splitting the fountain.' Two colors of ink were poured into the inkwell of the press from opposite ends. The inks blended slowly, creating a graduation of color across the sheet of paper as each one was printed. Each poster was slightly different from its predecessor, a distinction that was probably lost on the average supermarket shopper, but not on Sonnoli. The potential for individuality, resulting from chance combinations, is what most interested him as he prepared to undertake the new project.

'One thing that fascinates me is chance. Of course you have to guide it.'

FRONT

5	12	9	8
4	13	16	1

BACK

7	10	11	6
2	15	14	3

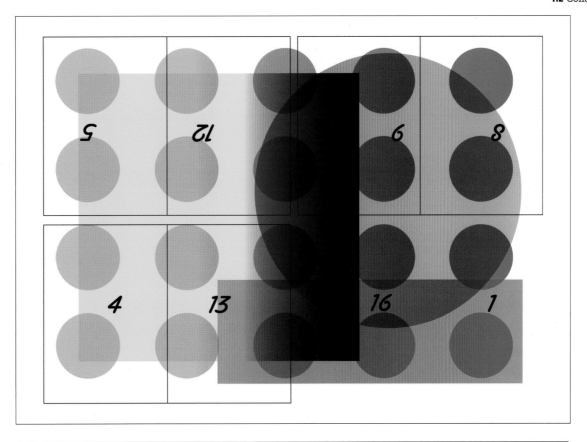

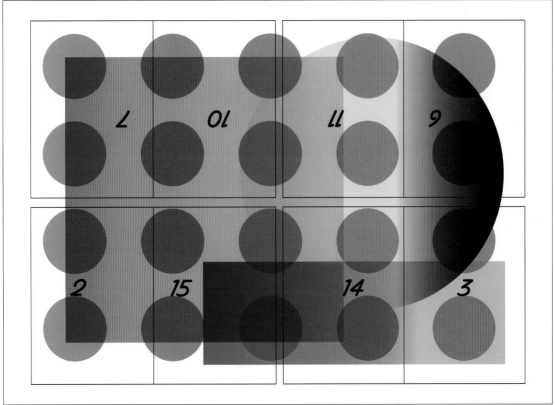

Facing page: The imposition layout (front and back) for the sixteen-page booklet determined the configuration in which the pages would be printed on the press sheet.

Above: Sonnoli's sketches helped him determine how the multiple graduated colors might be distributed using large-scale graphic elements.

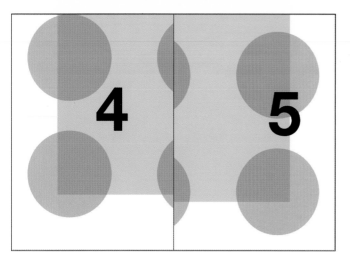

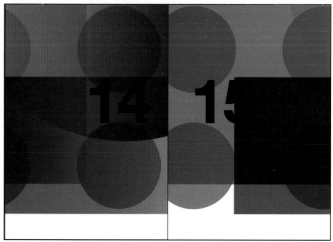

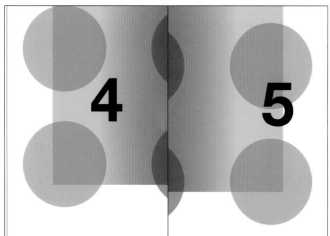

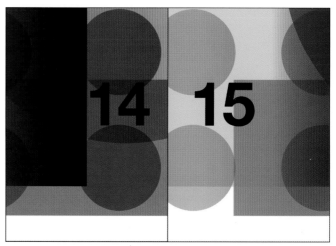

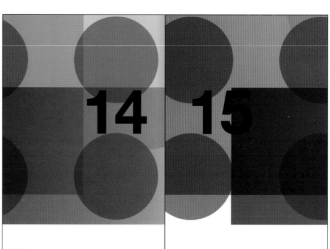

'I wanted to stay out of the design;
all the forms came from printing.'

Above: Sample pages created to illustrate how randomized color changes could be applied to different sections of the press sheet. Scale shifts, placement, and bright color create dramatic micro and macro compositions. Anticipating changes in color density was also a consideration as Sonnoli prepared these layouts.

Facing page: The visual language of Sonnoli's booklet originated from printer's registration marks, as well as test patterns that usually appear on the edges of a printer's press sheet.

The concept of chance had other precedents as well in Sonnoli's mind. He remembered the composer John Cage placing nuts, bolts, screws, and pieces of rubber between the strings of a grand piano in order to produce unexpected variations in the sound for his series of compositions for a prepared piano in the 1940s and 1950s. Designers like Karel Martens and others experimented with variations in printing during the 1960s. However, it was the work of the Italian poet and writer Nanni Balestrini and his experimental novel *Tristano*, published in 1964, that most captured Sonnoli's imagination.

Balestrini took his title from the medieval love story of the Cornish knight Tristan and the princess Isolde. The body of the novel was assembled from passages of text identical in length, following one another without any discernible clear logic. The passages, picked up from other texts, were collaged together without regard for time, place, action, or any traditional narrative form. By allowing each reader to independently form connections between the book's random texts, Balestrini created a unique and unexpected reading experience.

It was this possibility of producing an individual experience with a publication that prompted Sonnoli to consider his design carefully and create conditions that would promote, rather than eliminate, the possibility for 'happy accidents.' The content for the 6.75 x 9.5 inch (17 x 24 centimeter) sixteen-page booklet was at the discretion of the designer; Sonnoli elected to think in the abstract.

Because the client was a publisher, Sonnoli wanted to design something that was directly connected with the printing process. He decided to work with the registration marks, color bars, and calibration indicators that appear on the edges of each press sheet and are normally discarded when book pages are trimmed after printing. Sonnoli's idea was to enlarge these printer's marks and allow them to interact randomly with each other as the plate changes took place on the press during the four-color (cyan, magenta, yellow, and black) offset printing process. 'I didn't want to design something by hand,' he says, 'but to put the chance operation in play, using reproduction in a manufactured way.' Sonnoli made a decision to limit the text to just a brief introduction, allowing readers to focus on the intersections of forms and colors.

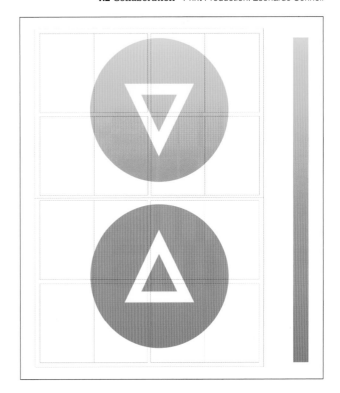

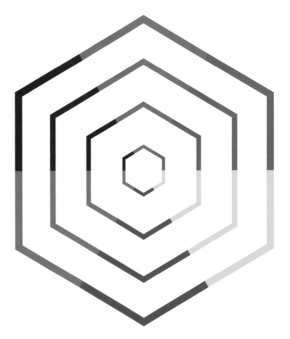

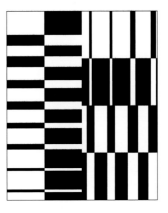

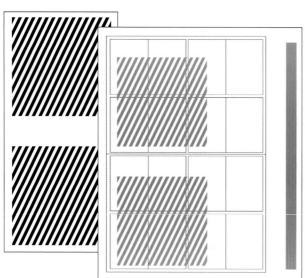

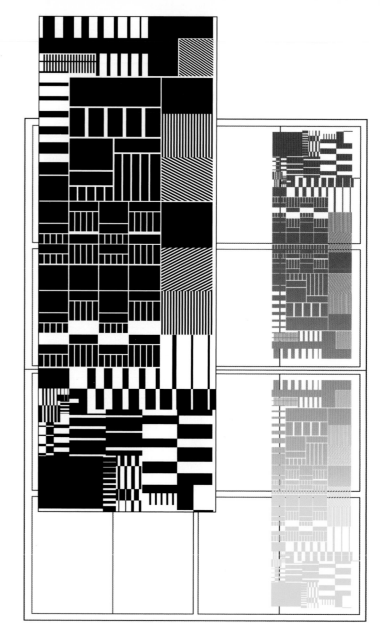

**'I really wanted to get an
unexpected result.'**

As a guide for the project, Sonnoli prepared a matrix of
interchangeable variables to suggest possible outcomes,
though he withheld from fixing any particular aspects
from the beginning. These 'sketches' allowed him to
move forward with confidence as he prepared the
final artwork.

He thought about graduation—colors blending over
a specified space—because it is always changing.
'Usually I don't use a lot of color. I work a lot in black and
white.' For this project he found that it was necessary to
use extreme color in order to emphasize the difference
in the graduations: 'I really wanted to get an unexpected
result.' His main idea was to produce, with an industrial
process—offset lithography in this case—about 1,500
booklets, each different from the other. 'That was the
idea of Nanni Balestrini: he wanted to do it with the text,
helped by the computer, combining the text in more than
2,000 different ways.'

Above: Mock-ups illustrating
how Sonnoli's black-and-
white graphic patterns would
be transformed by color
graduations. While some
color combinations could be
anticipated, only the actual
printing process would reveal
the final results.

Facing page: Sonnoli placed
the enlarged patterns
and registration marks on
sixteen-page press sheets,
then allowed the pressman
to rotate the plates randomly
during the printing process.

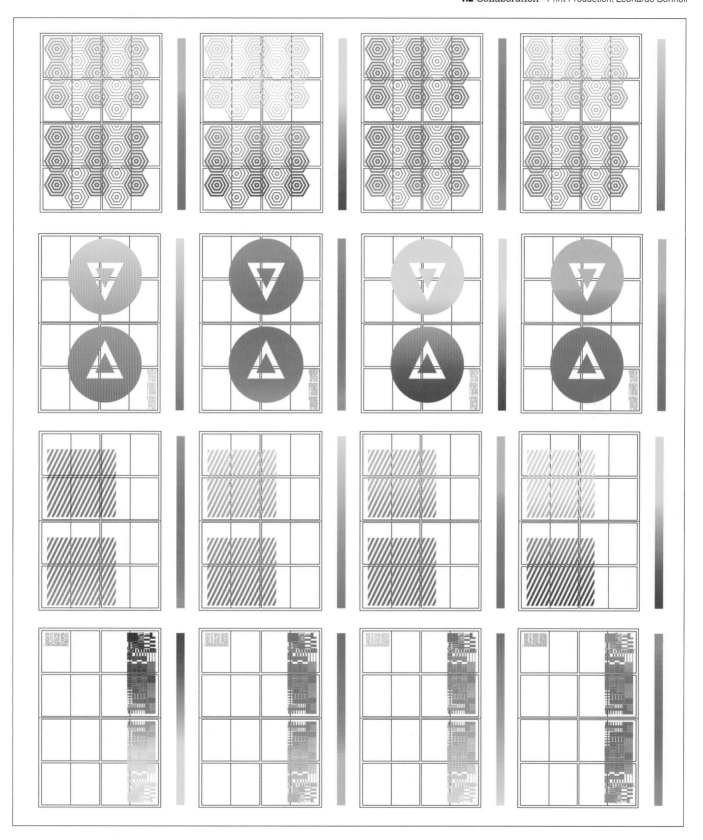

Even with meticulous planning, Sonnoli was sure that he had missed something, and wasn't totally confident about the final color combinations. The collaboration with the printer became very important. Upon seeing Sonnoli's design plan, the pressman informed him that with today's state-of-the-art computer-controlled presses, modifying the ink during the press run was not possible because the press would automatically compensate for any uneven distribution of ink in the fountain. Sonnoli didn't want to use the computer to manage the colors, so he had to find a work-around. Fortunately, one pressman remembered 'splitting' the fountain with a makeshift wooden divider, some years before. Sonnoli agreed that they should try this; a divider was created for the fountain, so that two different colors could be

placed side by side in the fountain at once, in order to allow them to gradually blend and achieve a range of color variations during the press run.

In addition to altering the colors in the fountain, the pressman changed the printing plates periodically throughout the process in order to randomize the combination of printed pages. Three different papers were rotated during the printing, one glossy and two uncoated, in both white and ivory. In the final stage of production, the printed press sheets were folded randomly so that the pages would be ordered differently. A small white sticker with the title of the book, the designer's name, and the name and address of Corraini Editions was then applied to designate the cover.

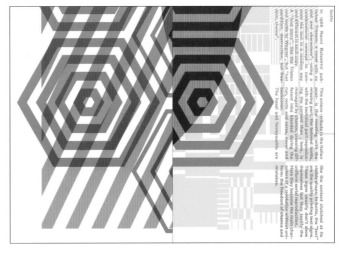

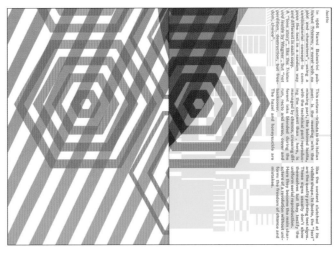
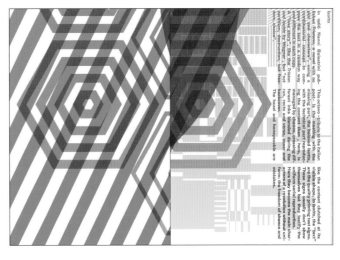

Printed pages of some of the final outcomes, illustrating how all the graphic elements and color combinations work harmoniously together.

Facing page: Two of the final press sheets, front and back, demonstrating the combination of graphic patterns, enlarged registration marks, text, and sample color graduations.

'If you put two consecutively printed copies next to each other,' Sonnoli says, 'they are very similar, but theoretically the graduation is always different.' Extreme differences can only be seen by comparing samples pulled from different parts of the print run.

As a final homage to Balestrini's *Tristano*, Sonnoli titled his booklet *Isotta* after the princess, Tristano's lost lover. He likes to think that by bringing Isotta to life as a companion to Tristano, there is a happy ending to the story.

'I didn't want to do something by hand; I wanted something repeated in an industrial way.'

171

'If you put two consecutive copies next to each other, they are very similar, but theoretically the graduation is always different.'

Top left: To achieve ideal combinations of colors for the final graduations, Sonnoli had the pressman divide the ink fountain using a makeshift wooden dam. The colors were changed several times during the press run in order produce random variations.

Above: Printed press sheets during production.

Facing page: Samples of Sonnoli's finished booklets, illustrating variations in color as well as paper stock.

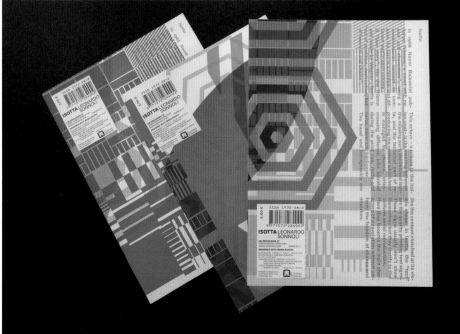

Creative DNA
Leonardo Sonnoli

Leonardo Sonnoli earned a diploma from the High Institute of Industrial Arts (ISIA), Urbino, and trained at the Tassinari/ Vetta Studio in Trieste. From 1990 to 2001, he worked for the Dolcini Associati Studio and then, along with Paolo Tassinari and Pierpaolo Vetta, founded CODEsign, becoming a partner in 2002. He designs visual identities for private and public companies, communication materials for cultural events, books, and informational and exhibition graphics.

Sonnoli has been awarded a Silver Medal by the Art Exhibition of Toyama, Japan, and received a Mention of Honour at the XIX Premio Compasso d'Oro/ADI. Other awards include the Merit Award of the Art Directors Club of New York, the special prize at the first China International Poster Biennial, and the Golden Bee award in Moscow. His posters are in a number of public and private collections, including the Bibliothèque nationale de France and the Musée des arts décoratifs, Paris, and the Museum of Design, Zurich. He exhibits his work around the world.

Sonnoli teaches art and design at the ISIA and the University of Venice, and has also taught workshops in numerous countries including the Netherlands, Turkey, Israel, France, and the United States.

Sonnoli is a member of the Alliance Graphique Internationale (AGI), and in 2003 was elected as its Italy President; he is a past member of the AGI International Executive Committee.

Stephen Fuller and Ahmet Ahmet

Title Sequence

'When I'm stuck working on a project, Saul Bass reminds me to keep it simple and get to the core of the idea.'

'It's always a fight to have the work appear effortless; effortlessness is sophisticated,' Stephen Fuller says. Maintaining this sense of effortlessness while capturing the emotions of war in the title sequence for HBO/Playtone's ten-episode series *The Pacific* would prove to be quite a challenge. Based in part on the books of Eugene Sledge (*With the Old Breed*) and Robert Leckie (*Helmet for My Pillow*) and the personal story of Medal of Honor recipient John Basilone, the series focuses on the United States Marine Corps battles with Japan in the Pacific theater during World War II, as seen through the eyes of these three main characters.

In an early communication to Fuller, executive producer Tom Hanks said that, through a discussion with a close friend, he had became aware of the work of WWII combat artists, and felt that an interpretation of their work might make an interesting basis for the title sequence. Taking this suggestion to heart, Fuller began by researching the wealth of visual material from that time period, examining drawings made by US soldiers, Japanese postcards, war posters, paintings, and a range of military maps. Fuller was also interested in the 'no nonsense' look of the typography used in original military documents.

Fuller and his team, designers Lauren Hartstone and Arisu Kashiwagi, at Imaginary Forces, New York, determined that drawings of the main characters based on stills from the series would occupy the largest share of screen time in the title sequence. Fuller's main concern, as he developed his drawing technique, was that the drawings would be too overworked: too much detail and they would not look like wartime sketches from the front lines; too little, and the sense of life so necessary in maintaining the emotional connection to the main characters could be completely lacking. Fuller continued to refine his techniques throughout the development of the project, ultimately producing thirty-three completed drawings.

This 1944 pencil drawing of a tank driver by Albert Gold was one of the inspirational drawings Fuller referred to during the research stage of the project.

Another important reference was this pencil drawing of a rifle company medic by Howard Brodie. This drawing appeared on the cover of *Yank* magazine in April 1945.

The broad range of material
collected by Fuller and his
team for an 'inspiration sheet'.

Two of Fuller's first sketches
as he started to define the
'look' for the title sequence.
The drawing at left illustrates
a frame grab from the film
Saving Private Ryan.

The design team began experimenting with graphite and charcoal, thinking it might function not only as a medium with which to represent the main characters, but also as a dark, symbolic gesture reflecting the drama of war. In their search for just the right effect, the designers tried breaking the charcoal sticks, scraping the edges across the paper, and spreading the dust across various surfaces in an abstract expressionist manner. High-speed close-up photography of charcoal slowly traveling across the surface of the paper in the act of drawing struck Fuller as an ideal way to combine two of the elements the team was looking for: the intensity of the war, and a sense of the battle locations. During five different sessions with variable-frame-rate cameras, Fuller and editor Corey Weisz captured the charcoal violently 'exploding' as it broke up, creating a fine graphite dust that looked like the black sand of the volcanic islands of the South

Pacific. The dark, fragile quality of the material and the gestures of the drawings would poetically capture the drama of war.

In structuring the sequence, the idea of a three-dimensional 'fly-through' appealed to Fuller at first, with the drawings being encountered, one at a time, in an open, expansive space. However, he dismissed this approach as being too 'effects-driven' and not in keeping with the time period being portrayed; he began instead to explore the idea of bringing the character portraits to life by transitioning from the drawings to live-action footage from the series. Additional live-action scenes would be incorporated to suggest the overall scope of the series. The key lay in combining the dramatic abstract nature of the charcoal close-ups, the representational portraits of the main characters, and selected footage from the series.

Fuller felt that his first board, 'Torn,' constructed of torn paper, was the most unique. He knew it pushed the form a bit too far, but he felt that it was a necessary step in the process.

'The challenge was how to make a title sequence emotionally impactful.'

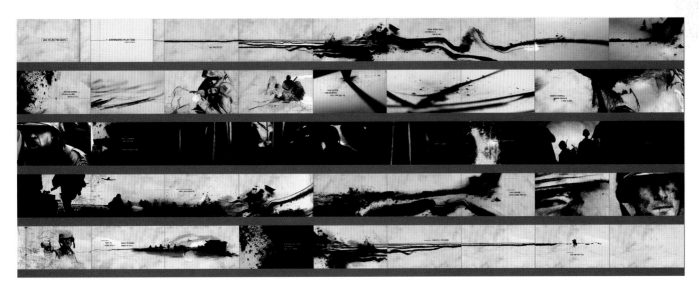

Top: Fuller's 'Line of Duty' story-board featured black and white chalk drawings on gray paper. With a softer contrast than the 'Torn' board, this concept allowed for clearer transition between drawn images and live-action footage.

Bottom: 'In Battle,' with its powerful red accents, captured the effortless but high-impact feeling Fuller was aiming for. This was the storyboard the producers accepted.

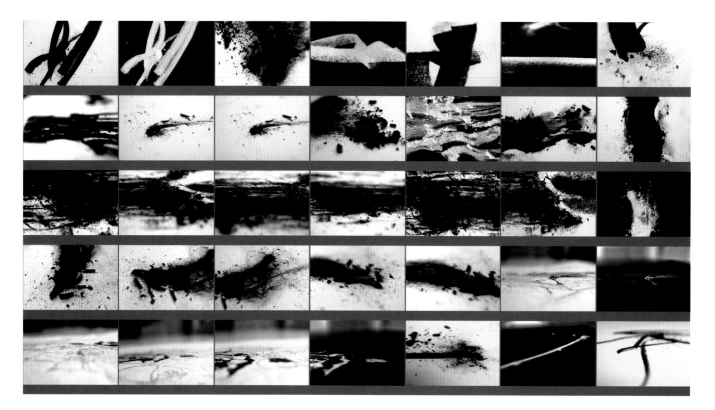

Contact sheet of frames from the initial charcoal and graphite tests Fuller and his team conducted in order to discover the limitations of close-up photography.

Fuller and his designers produced three storyboards to present to Playtone. The idea of the drawings combined with live-action footage was an active ingredient in all three proposals. Black and white would also be used for drama and emotional impact in all three boards; it was the density of the supporting structures within each board that varied.

Inspired by Saul Bass's titles and poster for the film *Bunny Lake Is Missing*, the first board, 'Torn,' used torn paper as a unifying element. Fuller knew this concept was pushing the limit of what the client might possibly accept, but he felt it was necessary in order to fully explore all the dramatic possibilities for the project. The second board, entitled 'Line of Duty,' was rendered in black and white chalk on gray paper, with softer contrast and clear transitions between the live-action components and the drawn renderings.

'In Battle,' the third board, featured charcoal drawings heightened with red accents. Fuller felt 'In Battle' captured the effortless feeling he was looking for and provided ample space for all of the drawing and live-action elements that would be needed to complete the sequence. Here again Fuller took his lead from Saul Bass's approach to design. Inspired by Bass's use of an iconic image and simple graphic elements, built up throughout a title sequence, Fuller's own sequence

started with just one simple horizontal line, suggesting both a horizon and the timeline of events unfolding in the series. As the line progressed, it fractured into three lines, symbolically representing the three main characters, and then continued to gain in complexity as the drawings appeared. The titles also ended with a single line, this time combined with the iconic image of one soldier carrying another. This board was accepted by Fuller's clients as the direction the final title sequence would take.

With the visual direction of the title sequence confirmed, Fuller, with his design team and editor, put together their first 'board-o-matic'—an animated storyboard—and began experimenting with possible music choices. At first, they envisioned something very contemporary that would successfully parallel the emotional feel of the drawing–live action combination, but in consultation with his clients, it was decided that Hans Zimmer, who composed the music for the series episodes, would also compose the score for the titles.

Zimmer's music delivered a highly emotional theme that expressed the pathos of World War II. The clients requested that certain emphases in the musical score be in alignment with 'high points' in the visuals. The team immediately went to work on merging all the visual elements—the drawn portraits, the macro photography

A selection of Fuller's drawings illustrating some of the scenes, including type treatment, that he and his designers considered for the final sequence.

of the charcoal, and the live-action footage from the series—with the music. The relationship between the musical and visual components became more tightly synchronized as they progressed. Fuller says, 'We started experimenting with the music and began to realize the true emotional power that can be achieved when music and image are successfully combined.'

Fuller continued to search for an iconic image with which to conclude the visual sequence. He decided to create mock-ups of film posters as a way to examine more closely the power of the fixed singular image. Using a variety of film posters as his guide—from Saul Bass's work to posters for more recent films like *The Mission* and *Miss Saigon*—Fuller carefully selected the strongest stills from the live-action footage and converted them into strong, resilient images. He wanted a powerful image for the ending of the titles and knew if he could identify it in poster form, it could work in the motion sequence as well. He finally settled on the image of one soldier carrying another.

In 1996 Saul Bass told *Film Quarterly* interviewer Pamela Haskins, 'My initial thoughts about what a title can do was to set the mood and the prime underlying core of the film's story, to express the story in some metaphorical way. I saw the title as a way of conditioning the audience, so that when the film actually began, viewers would already have an emotional resonance with it.' Fuller couldn't agree more. As he and his design team developed the first critical stages of this project, they always kept the 'emotional heart' of the narrative in mind so their audience would experience a truly authentic connection to the series.

With the initial development completed in New York by Fuller, the Los Angeles–based producers desired a closer collaboration, so Imaginary Forces moved the project to its Los Angeles office and into the hands of creative director Ahmet Ahmet. The initial brief was still firmly in place: create a synchronous, dramatic, and emotionally provocative title sequence. Ahmet knew that it was crucial to represent the characters not as 'gun-blazing' movie heroes, but as real-life people caught up in world events far beyond their control. The three primary concepts from Fuller's phase of the project would be retained: the character drawings and their transition to live footage, the charcoal close-ups, and the scenes of war from the series.

The first challenge for Ahmet and his team—producer Kathy Kelehan, editor Danielle White, and animators Chris Pickenpaugh and Jessica Sun—was to work toward locking the edit. Danielle reviewed all of the previous title edits and watched every episode of the series in search of emotional moments that could be featured in the titles. Working in Final Cut Pro, she would pull selected scenes from the series, mock up the transitions from drawing to live action, and give those clips to the animators to use as timing references.

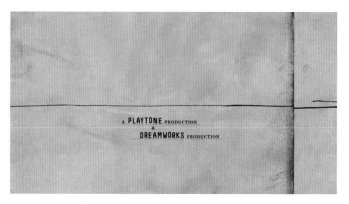

PRODUCTION DESIGNER
ANTHONY PRATT

SUPERVISING PRODUCERS
TIM VAN PATTEN
TERENCE WINTER

CO-EXECUTIVE PRODUCER TONY TO

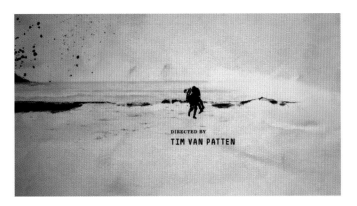

DIRECTED BY
TIM VAN PATTEN

Left: Still frames illustrating how the charcoal close-ups appeared in the title sequence. Overall line drawings, in combination with extreme close-ups, were used in order to intensify the feeling of combat.

Above: Four of the almost dozen posters Fuller created in his attempt to establish a single iconic image for the conclusion of the title sequence.

'If there is a rational reason, and you all understand what you're going for, you tend to be more successful in the collaboration.'

Maintaining the drawings as the centerpiece of the sequence was a challenge. The producers, Gary Goetzman and Tom Hanks, were keen to represent the main characters in a personal, introspective way, and to contrast that 'close-up' feeling with the larger situation of the war. For Ahmet, this meant creating additional drawings for the sequence to further extend Fuller's original concept and provide a more nuanced approach in their details that would then be used to maintain continuity throughout the entire title piece. Ahmet and his team completed another thirty or more drawings, always keeping in mind the idea that these images, while detailed, should nevertheless appear as if they had been created in the field by military sketch artists and not by a portrait artist in a formal studio setting. Another important condition that had been established from the first drafts of the project concerned the visual transitions from drawing to live-action footage of the primary characters. These transitions needed to appear as fluid as possible in order to avoid a clichéd 'line to film' look that could easily destroy the serious nature of the series.

The first task was to create a library of live-footage 'selects' from the A and B unit cameras. Then Ahmet and his design team would sketch out an idea using Adobe After Effects software and put it into the edit and present it to the producers for their feedback. Once approved, the final process would consist of creating a series of layered drawings by hand, with an emphasis on individual features, such as the eyes, nose, and mouth. In addition, each line or crosshatch effect would also be redrawn. All of these elements would be scanned for compositing in After Effects.

The use of slow-motion shots of the charcoal, in extreme close-up, presented another level of challenge for Ahmet and his team. The original high-speed clips were test shots from a consumer-grade digital camera and were only one-quarter of the full high-definition resolution (1920x1080 pixels) required for final delivery. While of some of the original shots, created in New York, could be brought up in size through the use of a software application, it was necessary to reshoot some of this material, as well as new shots Ahmet designed to help the editorial flow of the sequence. The producers signed off on a list of shots to be photographed by Ahmet and his director of photography Stacy Toyama using a slow motion Phantom camera at 300–400 fps (frames per second), a normal camera frame rate being 24 fps. This 'insert shoot' proved challenging due to the extreme amount of light required for properly exposing the image at such close range and also for the high speed. At one point the camera crashed and had to cool off for an hour—crucial shooting time was lost as the crew waited for it to recover. Getting the charcoal to 'perform' on camera also required much trial and error.

After Fuller and his design team completed the initial development of the project, they handed it over to creative director Ahmet Ahmet. Ahmet determined that more drawings were needed to fill out the sequence; these are four of the more than thirty additional drawings he then completed for the final sequence.

Below: Still frames illustrating a transition sequence from charcoal drawing to live film footage.

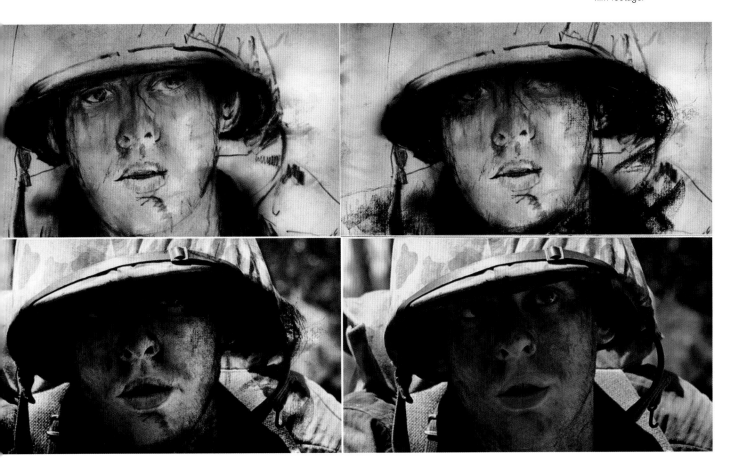

Ahmet developed new transitional treatments using live 'war' footage from the series, contrast enhanced, in combination with drawn, textured, and red color elements.

Facing page: Intimate close-up portraits transitioning from drawing to live footage within the title sequence.

The all-day shoot provided further choices from which to assemble the final edit. The slow-motion close-ups of shattering charcoal instilled a true sense of drama—like bombs bursting—while the addition of paper textures and blowing charcoal dust would add a further sense of continuity to the overall final sequence. This increased the level of detail and would meet the producers' requirements by making the entire sequence more emotional, more human. The producers were also interested in broadening the sense of scale within the piece. It was felt that adding more live-action footage to the final assembly would provide a backdrop against which the charcoal close-ups and the transitional portrait sequences could be placed, creating a 'push-pull' rhythm between more intimate moments and the larger, more dramatic situations represented in the war scenes. These shots—some of which were hand-selected by the producers—were treated with the same paper

texture and red painterly effects in order to unify them with the look of the rest of the sequence.

The final high-resolution renders were then imported into an Autodesk Inferno high-end compositing system. Ahmet worked closely with senior Inferno artist Rod Basham to conform the edited sequence and color correct the approved After Effects 'sketches' and add other discreet components—charcoal dust, paper textures, and title cards—to the final 'locked' footage.

The producers felt strongly that the creative efforts of both Stephen Fuller and Ahmet Ahmet had worked to successfully reveal the tone of the characters and provide their audience with an intense emotional atmosphere that would prepare them for the drama that would unfold in the finished series.

Creative DNA
Stephen Fuller
Ahmet Ahmet

Stephen Fuller is a graduate of the Fashion Institute of Technology's Graphic Design program. He helped start and develop the New York office of the creative studio Imaginary Forces, remaining eight years with the firm. As a design-based director, Fuller's expertise is integrating design and live action into the production process.

In September 2008, Fuller was awarded an Emmy for his title sequence for AMC's *Mad Men*. In 2010, his creative work on the title sequence for HBO's mini-series *The Pacific* and Showtime's *Nurse Jackie* earned him the honor of two Emmy nominations in the Outstanding Main Title Design category.

Fuller has also worked extensively in film and advertising, designing title sequences for such feature films as *The Mummy: Tomb of the Dragon Emperor*. He is currently a director of live action for the advertising industry in New York.

Ahmet Ahmet worked as a designer/director at the BBC in London for fourteen years, directing broadcast and design work for the promotions departments of BBC1 and BBC2. He also worked for CFC Framestore, where he headed up their first design department, working with filmmakers on special effects projects.

In 2000, Ahmet moved to the United States to work with Kyle Cooper at Imaginary Forces on the design of title sequences. Ahmet continues at Imaginary Forces in Los Angeles, where he works on a broad range of film and television projects.

To Nancy from Tom.
To Tom from Nancy.

Acknowledgments

First and foremost, we acknowledge with warmest thanks the brilliant designers who made this publication possible by sharing their extraordinary work and invaluable insights.

We owe a great deal to the LKP editorial team and thank them for giving their perceptive input every step of the way.

In addition we would like to credit our colleagues at the Rhode Island School of Design, who have been our steady mentors and friends, and the College for helping to support the project with a Faculty Development Grant.

Credits

1. Research

1.1 The Design Brief
A2/SW/HK
Turner Prize exhibition
Tate Britain, London, 2002–7
Spatial design, applied graphics, and print campaign
Design and art direction: A2/SW/HK (Scott Williams and Henrik Kubel)

Ergonomics—Real Design exhibition
Design Museum, London, 2009–10
Exhibition identity, applied graphics, and brochure, including bespoke display typeface
Design and art direction: A2/SW/HK (Scott Williams and Henrik Kubel)
Exhibition design: Michael Marriot
Photography: Luke Hayes and A2/SW/HK

1.2 Mapping/Modeling
Dubberly Design Office
A Model of the Creative Process
Written and designed by Hugh Dubberly and Shelley Evenson

A Model of Brand
Written and designed by Hugh Dubberly

Java Technology Concept Map
Written and designed by Audrey Crane, Paul Devine, Harry Saddler, Jim Faris, and Hugh Dubberly

1.3 The Client
Johnson Banks
Logos, various clients
Johnson Banks developed Christian Aid's Poverty Over visual identity based on an original idea.
Commission for Architecture and the Built Environment – CABE is now part of the Design Council www.designcouncil.org.uk

Pew Center for Arts & Heritage identity
Creative Director: Michael Johnson
Designers: Michael Johnson and Pali Palavathanan

Think London identity
Creative Director: Michael Johnson
Designers: Michael Johnson, Julia Woollams, and Paola Faoro
© London & Partners

Anthony Nolan identity and posters
Creative Director: Michael Johnson
Designers: Michael Johnson and Julia Woollams
© Copyright Anthony Nolan. Charity registration number 803716/SC038827

2. Inspiration

2.1 Found Objects
Melle Hammer and Yara Khoury
'Typographic Matchmaking in the City'
Khatt Foundation, the Netherlands
Kasheeda-latin and Kasheeda-arabic 3D typefaces

2.2 Materials
Graphic Thought Facility
'Mirror Mirror'
V&A Enterprises, 2006

Mighty Productions identity

Marks & Spencer Café Revive identity

Tord Boontje by Martina Margetts
Published by Rizzoli International, 2007

54th Carnegie International exhibition
Carnegie Museum of Art, Pittsburgh, 2004–5
Logo, graphics, and exhibition catalog
Overall exhibition design: Michael Maltzen Architecture

Who am I? exhibition
Science Museum, London, 2000
Object-labeling system
Overall exhibition design: Casson Mann

Who am I? exhibition
Science Museum, London, 2010
Object-labeling system
Overall exhibition design: Casson Mann
Interactive design: AllofUs

2.3 Collage
Skolos Wedell
2010 Lyceum Traveling Fellowship in Architecture poster
Lyceum Fellowship Committee

2.4 Synaesthesia
James Goggin
Wire magazine covers:
#274, December 2006: Photo by Kareem Black. Art direction by James Goggin.
#279, May 2007: Photo by Leon Chew. Art direction by James Goggin

Wire Tapper CD covers:
Wire Tapper 16: Ilustration: Distorted Rectangle pattern by Richard Rhys. Art direction by James Goggin
Wire Tapper 17: Illustration: Ink and Pen patterns by Samuel Nyholm/Reala. Art direction by James Goggin
Wire Tapper 18: Illustration: Penjet patterns by Jaan Evart, Julian Hagen, and Daniël Maarleveld. Art direction by James Goggin.

Space Patterns (*Univers*, *Mars*, *All-Star*)
Draft magazine, October 2004

Docklands Light Railway Public Arts Programme logo, brochure, and poster
Docklands Light Railway/ Transport for London

Unilever Series: Olafur Eliasson poster
Tate Modern, London, 2003
© Tate, London 2011

The Family Beds by Alison Turnbull
Published by Ruskin School of Drawing and Fine Art, University of Oxford, 2005

3. Drawing

3.1 Thumbnails
Michel Bouvet
Oxu poster
La Pépinière théâtre, Paris

Hamlet poster
Théâtre Les Gémeaux, Sceaux, France
Designer: Michel Bouvet
Photographer: Francis Laharrague

3.2 Sketchbooks
Ed Fella
Sketchbooks

Announcement flyer for *Two Lines Align: Drawings and Graphic Design by Ed Fella and Geoff McFetridge* at the Gallery at REDCAT, Los Angeles, 2008
Design: Ed Fella

T-shirt
Designed for the American Institute of Graphic Arts Student Conference, California Institute of the Arts, 2010

3.3 Type Design
Cyrus Highsmith
The Font Bureau, Inc.
Daley's Gothic, Biscotti, and Relay typefaces; sketchbooks

All typefaces copyright Cyrus Highsmith, published by the Font Bureau, Sketchbooks copyright Cyrus Highsmith

4. Narrative

4.1 Book Design
Lorraine Wild
Green Dragon Office
John Baldessari: Pure Beauty exhibition catalog
Los Angeles County Museum of Art
Published by Prestel Publishing, 2009

Martin Kippenberger: The Problem Perspective exhibition catalog
Museum of Contemporary Art, Los Angeles
Published by the MIT Press, 2008

4.2 Virtual Models
Me Company
Kenzo Autumn/Winter 2001 collection advertising campaign
Images by Me Company
© Me Company 2001

5. Abstraction

5.1 Symbol Design
Ahn Sang-Soo
Life Peace Logo
Life Peace Organization (Korea)

5.2 Type as Image
Ralph Schraivogel
LIVE/EVIL poster
Designed for Sacha Wigdorovits, 2008
Extract from *Against Apathy and Forgetfulness* by Sacha Wigdorovits used with permission

5.3 Identity
Michael Bierut
New World Symphony identity
Michael Bierut, Pentagram

6. Development

6.1 Iteration
Philippe Apeloig
Studio Philippe Apeloig
L'Asie des ecritures croisées, un vrai roman
Fête du livre, Aix-en-Provence, 2007

Wole Soyinka—La maison et le monde
Fête du livre, Aix-en-Provence, 2007

6.2 Systems
Anette Lenz and Vincent Perrottet
La Géode poster
La Géode Omnimax cinema, Paris
Atelier Anette Lenz

Mois du Graphisme exhibition poster
Echirolles, France, 2006–7
Atelier Anette Lenz

Théâtre de Rungis posters
Théâtre de Rungis, Paris, 2000–2001
Atelier Anette Lenz

Théâtre d'Angoulême promotional materials
Joel Günzburger, Théâtre d'Angoulême
Concept and creation: Anette Lenz and Vincent Perrottet
Photographer: Myr Muratet

7. Collaboration

7.1 Programming
Ben Fry
Fathom Information Design
Genomic Cartography: Chromosome 21;
Genomic Cartography: Chromosome 18;
Aligning Humans and Mammals, illustration for *Seed* magazine, December 2007;
Linking, illustration for *New York* magazine, February 20, 2006
© Ben Fry

Nuage Vert
HeHe, Helsinki, 2008

Cell Cycle
Nervous System, 2009

7.2 Print Production
Leonardo Sonnoli
Isotta, Un Sedicesimo 17
Design and art direction: Leonardo Sonnoli in collaboration with Irene Bacchi
Published by Corraini Edizioni, 2010
© Leonardo Sonnoli

7.3 Title Sequence
Stephen Fuller and Ahmet Ahmet
The Pacific title sequence
Home Box Office, Inc. (HBO)/Playtone

Imaginary Forces, New York Office:
Stephen Fuller, Director/Creative Director and Illustrator
Lauren Hartstone, Senior Designer
Corey Weisz, Editor
Arisu Kashiwagi, Designer
Cara McKenny, Producer

Imaginary Forces, Los Angeles Office:
Ahmet Ahmet, Creative Director
Kathy Kelehan, Producer
Danielle White, Editor
Chris Pickenpaugh and Jessica Sun, Animators

Photos from HBO/Playtone's ten-episode mini-series *The Pacific*